THE
WRY ROMANCE
OF THE
LITERARY RECTORY

DEBORAH ALUN-JONES

THE
WRY ROMANCE
OF THE
LITERARY RECTORY

with 75 illustrations, 12 in colour

For Jeremy, Tom, Ben, Ed and Hugo

Frontispiece The Old Rectory, Farnborough,
John Betjeman's home, 1945–51

First published in the United Kingdom
in 2013 by Thames & Hudson Ltd,
181A High Holborn, London WC1V 7QX

British Library Cataloguing-in-Publication Data
A catalogue record for this book is available from
the British Library

ISBN 978-0-500-51677-5

Printed and bound in China
by C & C Offset Printing Co. Ltd

To find out about all our publications, please
visit **www.thamesandhudson.com**. There you
can subscribe to our e-newsletter, browse
or download our current catalogue, and buy any
titles that are in print.

CONTENTS

Illustration from *The Writings of Gilbert White of Selborne*, 1938, by Eric Ravilious.

The Last Outpost
of Time Past

I T WAS 1947, and in a small inner hall of a newly decommissioned old rectory on the Berkshire Downs some friends were crowded around an upright piano for a little post-dinner musical entertainment. As Charles Coborn's 'Two Lovely Black Eyes' resounded through the house, the rationing and austerity of these postwar years were momentarily forgotten. Within the walls of the elegant, if spartan, rectory, layers of past certainties offered a firm platform upon which to face a future that threatened rapid change.

The building had been bought at auction on VE Day two years earlier by that great celebrator of Englishness John Betjeman. From here, with his friend the artist John Piper, he would continue the mapping and fixing of his vision of England that had begun in the 1930s with the first Shell Guides to particular counties, aimed at the new motoring public. Theirs was an ongoing campaign to record for a nation whose foundations were shifting a vision of the past rooted in its landscape and historic buildings. They were not alone. From H. V. Morton's *In Search of England* (1927) onwards there had been a spate of literary enthusiasm for the re-examination of village life. Edmund Blunden's *The Face of England* (1932), J. B. Priestley's *English Journey* (1934) and H. J. Massingham's *The English Countryside* (1939) all contributed to this narrative of parochial rediscovery. In the same period, T. S. Eliot reworked the physical locations of Burnt Norton, East Coker and Little Gidding into his poetic exploration of time and place, *Four Quartets* (1935–42). Virginia Woolf, writing at Monk's House, Rodmell, deep in the Sussex countryside, was also attuned to voices from the rural past, conjuring up an image of the cleric and naturalist Gilbert White of Selborne escaping from the eighteenth century and 'winging his way to us in the dusk along the hedgerows'.

In his desire to live a life in the Old Rectory at Farnborough that was steeped in the past, Betjeman was drawing on a long tradition of writers who have been associated with clerical livings. The novels of Jane Austen, the most famous of rectory daughters, established the myth of 'the unpretending comfort of a well-connected parsonage' that Catherine Morland, the heroine of *Northanger Abbey* (1817), dreams about. The parsonage is portrayed as a civilized and civilizing influence but there was another side to such supposed parsonic perfection. Even in Austen's world there are examples of clerics not quite so worthy of our estimation: Mr Collins in *Pride and Prejudice* (1813) is an over-mannered, absurdly obsequious example.

It is in the Yorkshire village of Haworth, however, that a darker romantic vision of rectory living is rooted, in the unremarkable stone structure on the edge of the moors that nurtured the genius of the Brontë family. Living conditions for the Brontës at Haworth Parsonage were far harsher than anything presented in Austen's drawing rooms. 'I can hardly tell you how time gets on at Haworth,' Charlotte wrote to her friend Ellen Nussey in 1845. 'There is no event whatever to mark its progress. One day resembles another, and all have heavy, lifeless physiognomies.' Charlotte had no time for Austen's rarefied circles: 'I should hardly like to live with her ladies and gentlemen in their genteel but confined houses.' The Brontës' landscape was a more rugged imaginative terrain, 'moorish and wild', as Charlotte described the setting of *Wuthering Heights* (1847) in her editor's preface to the 1850 edition of her sister's novel.

Motherless and with an eccentric and somewhat distant father, Charlotte saw two sisters die before she was 10. She and her surviving younger sisters, Emily and Anne, and their troubled brother, Branwell, created their own world within Haworth Parsonage. From an early age, the children composed tales set in the fictional realms of Glass Town and Angria, stories whose pages were hand-stitched together and read aloud while pacing around the dining-room table. The Brontë sisters would go on in adulthood to create their own brand of romantic heroine, set outside the norms of fashionable society; plain yet unconventional Jane Eyre and the savage Catherine Earnshaw were unexpected narrative creations from the daughters of a remote clerical home. They stand in

'I feel as if we were all buried here,' Charlotte Brontë wrote of Haworth Parsonage.

sharp contrast to Austen's more mannered domestic creatures, just as Haworth Parsonage, overlooking the seeping gloom of a brimming graveyard with the wild moors beyond, embodies the bleaker side of the comfortable notion of parsonage living that is central to Austen's fiction and which she herself experienced in the fine family rectories at Adlestrop and Ashe.

For centuries, British rectories (or parsonages), vicarages and their rather grander cousins, chanceries, have offered their clerical inhabitants the protection of an ordered environment, infused with the rhythms of the Church seasons and the poetic language of the King James's Bible and the Book of Common Prayer. So it is unsurprising that eight Poet Laureates have emerged from the rectory, from John Dryden to Cecil Day-Lewis, and including Alfred, Lord Tennyson. Tennyson and his siblings sought refuge from their troubled father in the attic rooms of the rectory at Somersby, Lincolnshire, where they escaped into other, interior worlds and shadowy sequestered places. Incumbents and their children experienced what often proved to be a particularly creative form of isolation. This was certainly true for Laurence Sterne (1713–68), perpetual curate of Coxwold in North Yorkshire. There, in his 'philosophical retreat', he wrote most of the first comic novel in the English language, *The Life and Opinions of Tristram Shandy, Gentleman* (1759–67).

Daughters of a clerical household often had access to knowledge and libraries long before female education was considered desirable or was generally available. The novelist Elizabeth Gaskell, Charlotte Brontë's biographer, was the product of such an upbringing. As for the Brontës themselves, their learning, combined with their solitude, enabled them to explore places that Charlotte's heroine Jane Eyre referred to as 'recesses in my mind which would be only mine'; this resulted in some of the finest novels in English literature. Similarly, as a child, the detective-story writer Dorothy L. Sayers retreated to her third-floor nursery at Bluntisham Rectory near Huntingdon to construct her own fictional realm and was so well educated by her father and governesses that she gained the Gilchrist Scholarship to Somerville College, Oxford, in 1912.

For many people, the idyllic rural home is epitomized by the gracious façade of the rectory or parsonage. Traditionally, the term 'rectory' meant the home of the rector (from 'ruler') who, as the incumbent, was entitled to the tithes of the parish. Where a rector was absent, a vicar (from the Latin *vicarius*, 'substituted') was housed in the parish in his stead. His home was the vicarage and, since he received the smaller tithes or was paid a stipend, the building was usually of lesser status. Since tithes have long been abolished, such ecclesiastical distinctions are now purely historical, and in this book I have used the general term 'rectory' to describe these village homes with such romantic associations.

A picture of serenity and restrained civility, the buildings sit close to the church they were constructed to serve. No pastoral scene is complete without the faded solidity of the village rectory. These unpretentious edifices, so central to the national spirit, have stood firm against the spiritual and temporal storms that have beset rural parishes through the centuries. They have survived the onslaughts of the Reformation, the Civil War, the Restoration and the Glorious Revolution, the rise of Dissenters, the mid-Victorian crisis of faith, and latterly the threat posed by the increasingly secular nature of society.

The building now regarded as the quintessential rectory is usually a Georgian affair. This was the period when the gentleman churchman flourished, since many of them were the younger sons of upper-class families, and there was a spate of clerical house-building. A series of Residence Acts required priests to live in their parishes (rather than pocket the tithes and live elsewhere) and a gentleman rector would require an abode commensurate with his status. These were a far cry from the earliest rectories, which were simple halls on a par with the homes of the local yeomen farmers.

At the Dissolution of the Monasteries, when Church lands – representing half of the country's wealth – were confiscated by the Crown, the landed classes relished the prospect of having benefices and the related incomes in their gift, as letters from the petitioning aristocracy show. The Duke of Norfolk, although unwilling to seem 'pushful', felt 'that where others speak I must speak too' and in a letter to the King's chief minister Thomas Cromwell he asked for the livings of Bungay and Woodbridge. Meanwhile, the Archbishop of Canterbury, Thomas Cranmer, had his eye on a living for his brother-in-law and felt that 'Shefford would suit'. Henry VIII's survey (Valor Ecclesiasticus, 1535) showed, however, that such rich livings were far from the norm, with half of the 9,000 benefices valued at less than £10 a year, at a time when a craftsman would have earned £8 per annum.

In the majority of parishes, the parsonage would not have been a dwelling of particular distinction or size, but circumstances had now changed. The parish priest was no longer just in charge of disseminating church teachings to his parishioners and conducting services, he was also part of the Church of England, a social and political as well as spiritual force, and his house would need to combine these functions and to declare the same. It had to present a particular public face to the parish; here was the fulcrum on which rural society turned.

There were changing practical considerations, too. After the Reformation, the priest could be married. There were children and a household, all of whom needed to be accommodated. He was also increasingly likely to be educated. To succeed on a political as well as spiritual level the priest must be respected, a figure of status in the community. Outside the reach of the central forces of government, the parish priest administered justice and welfare, sometimes in the role of Justice of the Peace, a post held by Sydney Smith, the early nineteenth-century essayist and wit, and rector at Foston in Yorkshire.

As many benefices or livings were held in plurality by the same man, however, parishes were often abandoned to the occasional ministrations of a curate; social and spiritual order, along with the parsonage house, was left to decay. This was the case in the 1630s for the poet-rector George Herbert at Bemerton, where the rectory needed substantial work before it was fit for habitation, because his predecessor had preferred to live in a more desirable parsonage over twenty miles away.

George Herbert regarded his fellow country clergy with contempt and set out to redeem and redefine the role of the rural parson. The parsonage itself was a vital part of this redefinition. He believed his house should reflect order, cleanliness and self-discipline. He aimed for this at Bemerton and succeeded, but the Civil War and the Interregnum halted any widespread adoption of his vision. The devastation of war caused extensive dislocation in the parishes, with many livings sequestered by Oliver Cromwell and the Commonwealth and the resident priests either killed or thrown out of their rectories. These clerical homes were then neglected, as most parishes had no money for rebuilding and the owners of the livings were similarly financially stretched. Gregory King's 1688 analysis of English society puts lesser clergymen (parish priests) just above farmers on the social scale but still far below the level of 'gentleman' and, at £45, on a sixth of his annual income.

The number of pluralist incumbents meant that the many curates who were graduating in greater numbers from universities often had no clerical home or means of financial support. They were reduced to wandering from parish to parish, subsisting rather than living, or becoming chaplains to wealthy families where they were treated like servants. A Revd Richard Steele complained in 1728 that he found his patron and his lady 'very sullen and out of humour' as he had kept his place at table rather than offering to rise at the second course as a lowly curate should. He compounded his social crime by helping himself to a jelly, far too frivolous a food for a man of the cloth, and he was dismissed the following day.

Itinerant curates and absentee parish priests had an adverse effect on the standing of the Church of England in rural communities. Resident country clergy with low incomes also contributed to the Church's dilapidated image, reflected in a residence that they could ill afford to maintain. This was recognized and to some extent resolved by the Queen Anne's Bounty Act of 1703, the first of several, which augmented the livings of the most impoverished clergy and allowed the governors of the fund to award grants for the repair and construction of parsonages. Another way for the clergy to improve their homes, as well as their social and financial status, was by marrying well. Alton Barnes Rectory in Wiltshire was rebuilt in 1718 using funds acquired in this way and the work was commemorated in a stained-glass window in the church.

By 1752 William Halfpenny, in his *Useful Architecture in Twenty-one New Designs for Country Parsonages, Farm Houses and Inns,* was recommending designs for the parsonage building and rebuilding that had resulted from a resurgence in religious fervour accompanied by good harvests and increasing tithe incomes, as well as the financial support available from Queen Anne's Bounty. The Clergy Residences Repair Act (1776), known as Gilbert's Act, further facilitated the 'speedy and effectual building, rebuilding, repairing or purchasing' of the clerical dwelling. The rural rector's abode now proclaimed his status as a gentleman. This coincided with the rise of the cult of the aesthetic and many parsonages of the period reflect the fashion for improvement. The eighteenth-century poet William Cowper noted with dismay the country clergyman's preoccupation with his home, sometimes at the expense of his church:

> I could not help wishing that the honest vicar, instead of indulging
> his genius for improvements, by enclosing his gooseberry bushes
> with a Chinese rail, and converting half an acre of his glebe land
> into a bowling-green, would have applied part of his income to
> the more laudable purpose of sheltering his parishioners from the
> weather during their attendance on divine service.

Jane Austen, however, approved of the clergyman's efforts, as her description of the village of Uppercross in *Persuasion* (1818) suggests:

> [A place] containing only two houses superior in appearance to those of the yeomen and labourers: the mansion of the squire, with its high walls, great gates, and old trees, substantial and unmodernized, and the compact, tight parsonage, enclosed in its own neat garden, with a vine and a pear tree trained round its casements.

Within such a building, the rector would need a study or a library, his own contemplative space where he could retreat to write his sermons and pursue his personal enthusiasms away from public exposure. Church finances were not, however, unlimited. Livings in rural parishes depended on tithes, and agricultural productivity levels fluctuated according to the size of the harvest, which was reflected in the price of corn. If he was a pragmatic man, the rector would often supplement his income by taking in pupils, another pressure on internal accommodation. As a result, the high aesthetic of the rectory's exterior was often not matched by the interior. Rooms were smaller and the conditions more crowded than the outside suggested. This put its own stresses on life in the parsonage. For the man who did not relish living in an isolated parish it must have been more of a prison, and a cramped one at that, from which he must present an ordered and controlled front.

The genteel world of the rural rectory in its circumscribed domain was Austen's idealized reality, a presented fiction for one who had spent her whole life in a network of rectories, and not all of them as comfortable as that awaiting Edmund Bertram in *Mansfield Park* (1814). Whatever his degree of affluence, the educated rector was, however, a gentleman and in the early to mid-nineteenth century still held a pivotal position in the community. Austen may have mocked the aspirational clerical couple of Mrs Elton and her 'caro sposo' in *Emma* (1815), but she accepted, along with most of society, that the country clergy occupied a central role in the social and religious structures that bound communities. Parishioners were still inclined to bow to Church influence and the rectory emanated spiritual and moral propriety, as yet untroubled by the full force of late Victorian doubt.

Nonetheless the world was changing. Although the Church attempted to maintain its patriarchal authority in the parishes through the several Acts of

Residence, it was a fight for the hearts and minds of a nation that was in some ways already lost. There were other social pressures for change; suffrage was extending, the improved communication provided by the railway resulted in an inexorable move away from the countryside to the expanding cities and the inevitable erosion of traditional ties between the Church and the agrarian community. The unpopular payment of tithes came under scrutiny, too, and the Tithe Acts, introduced and amended throughout the nineteenth century (although tithes would not be entirely abolished until an act of 1936), contributed to this severing of long-established links. The Welsh Church Act (1914), disestablishing the Church of England in the principality and creating a separate Church in Wales, dealt the unravelling parish model a further blow.

George Eliot, in her stories *Scenes of Clerical Life* (1857), had already written about the social and cultural implications of religious reform and the rise of the Dissenters, lamenting the demise of the avuncular parson who 'smoked very long pipes and preached very short sermons'. Such a vision had been swept away on a tide of industrial progress and she viewed its passing with sadness. A few years later, in 1865, Anthony Trollope, whose grandfathers were both clergymen, found the crisis of structure and faith in the Church an appropriate target for satirical examination in his series of essays 'Clergymen of the Church of England'. Yet even as the rectory and all it represented was crumbling, the literary myth endured, and was perpetuated by Trollope himself in his fictional Barsetshire parishes.

Charles Darwin, the man most responsible for the Victorian crisis of faith, was not immune to the attractions of living in such a building; he was nurtured by the silence and serenity of Down House, the old rectory at Downe in rural Kent, where he moved in 1842. Here, in the same study that had inspired countless clerical compositions, he struggled with his own faith while writing *On the Origin of Species* (1859), the book that would shake the foundations of the Church of England. Twenty miles away at Higham, Charles Dickens moved into Gad's Hill, the former vicar's home, which he bought in 1856, establishing his social rather than spiritual status. *Great Expectations* (1861) was written in its book-lined study.

This genre of building has provided the *genius loci* for many writers and artists, the bricks and mortar offering a level of protection against the sense of dislocation often experienced beyond the rectory walls. This was true for Anglican and atheist alike. The poet Rupert Brooke, although in very different

Charles Darwin's study at Down House, Kent, the former rectory where he wrote
On the Origin of Species (1859).

Rupert Brooke in the garden of the Old Vicarage, Grantchester, 1911.

circumstances, since he was at the beginning of his career, also found inspiration in his clerical home. A declared 'agnogger', or agnostic, he thought it the perfect 'fit' for writing what he called 'my kind of poetry'. His poem 'The Old Vicarage, Grantchester', written while in spiritual and physical exile in Berlin in 1912, captures the England of tea and honey on the lawn, the church clock standing guard, parish and pastoral harmony stilled for eternity in this moment with the vicarage at its heart. This spirit finds echoes in Edward Thomas's poem 'Adlestrop' (1917) – 'And willows, willow-herb, and grass, / And meadow-sweet, and haycocks dry' – an evocation of pastoral England Jane Austen might almost have recognized from her window when staying with her cousin at Adlestrop Rectory in the 1790s (Thomas's view was from a resting train). For the two poets, writing in the second decade of the twentieth century, the simplicity of English village life with rural certainties at its core represented an image of England that would stand firm, untouched by the horrors of the war.

The literary legacy of the rectory continued on in the twentieth century despite the decline of the twin parish pillars of Church and State. Many writers responded by seeking inspiration within the peaceable enclosure of the parish and a clerical abode. The parochial life attracted writers such as Virginia Woolf, whose last novel, *Between the Acts* (1941), written at Monk's House, the Woolfs' home bordering the church and graveyard at Rodmell, was set in an English village. The vicar's residence itself was chosen by Agatha Christie as the location for *Murder at the Vicarage* (1930) and George Orwell for *A Clergyman's Daughter* (1935). Dorothy L. Sayers used the trope of the safe, ordered parish and turned it on its head to make it the place of malevolent imaginings in one of her detective stories. John Betjeman appropriated the consoling construct of parish living at Farnborough Old Rectory after the Second World War and in the same period, in the depths of Wales, the poet-rector R. S. Thomas pursued his quest for an authentic poetic voice while striding the hills above his clerical home. Ted Hughes and Sylvia Plath were seduced briefly by life in an old thatched vicarage in a village near Okehampton in Devon, until the vision was distorted and the peaceful graveyard took on a more menacing aspect as 'the wall of old corpses' in Plath's poem 'Letter in November' (1962).

Even in the twenty-first century, although the rectory's clerical inhabitants may have long gone, the buildings themselves echo with what John Ruskin called the 'voicefulness' of their past literary residents. This is exemplified by the old rectory at Bemerton, near Salisbury, where a contemporary novelist and

Virginia Woolf at Monk's House, Rodmell, in the 1930s. Woolf relished the position of the house at the centre of the parish, 'with the grey extinguisher of the church steeple pointing my boundary,' as she noted in her diary.

poet – Vikram Seth – now lives in what were George Herbert's 'rooms of verse'. Life in the present is necessarily informed and enhanced by the lives of past generations and the rectory embodies that continuing discourse. The de Waal children, when they lived in the Chancery at Lincoln during the early 1970s, were very conscious of the creative Benson family who had inhabited the building a century earlier.

This book explores the hidden stories behind the ordered façade of these much-loved buildings through the lives of some of the literary figures who have lived and worked in them. For those who resided behind the walls of such declared parsonic perfection was it possible or even desirable to strive to match the presented ideal? Or was the disjunction between public image and private reality an ideal space for creativity – where the irreconcilable could be reconciled in fiction, poetry and art? Perhaps this is one of the reasons why so many writers are connected to these comparatively unassuming houses.

Maybe more than any other domestic building these structures mirror the stereotype of the national psyche: the cool, calm exterior concealing the turbulence and drama of the inner self. 'Solus' was the one word carved on the wall of a tiny rectory in Northumberland in 1832 by the marooned incumbent, an ex-naval officer, and it speaks volumes for his lonely plight. Such isolation took its toll on some who, like Branwell Brontë at Haworth, imbibed opiates to numb the pain of disassociation. Others, such as the Revd Sydney Smith, found reserves with which to face their exile with humour and courage. For many, time in the rectory was an intensely creative experience as minds turned inwards in extreme self-absorption. Eccentrics abound alongside literary geni-uses: the Very Revd William Buckland (1784–1856) decided to serve his god by eating his way through the animal kingdom. Others, such as the Revd Jack Russell (1795–1883), whose name lives on in the breed of terrier he favoured, preferred to lead their flock from the hunting field.

Today, the rectory remains an enduring symbol of continuity against the darker forces of commercialism, urbanism, and aesthetic and moral decay. Here is a repository for a mystical spirit of England, a recognizable rootedness in the village landscape that reflects back to us a timeless sense of identity. The yearn-ing for a feeling of belonging remains entwined with the image of life in a rural rectory. With the increased secularization of society, amalgamation of parishes and resulting sale of Church property, however, the rectory is now more likely to be a postwar construction than the lyrical buildings of the imagination. Yet its romance still holds sway, even if it is now 'The Old Rectory'. And if, as Virginia Woolf pointed out in her essay 'Two Parsons', where she discussed the diaries of the eighteenth-century Parson Woodforde, it is all a fiction, what of it?

Still, if it is a dream, let us indulge it a moment longer. Let us believe that some things last, and some places and some people are not touched by change. On a fine May morning, with the rooks rising and the hares scampering and the plover calling among the long grass, there is much to encourage the illusion. It is we who change and perish. Parson Woodforde lives on … the house, thank God, withstands the storm; and then again there is the first swallow, and Parson Woodforde takes his greyhounds out a-coursing.

This is the story from both sides of the rectory door, the romantic exterior and the secret interior life. As we grope blindly towards a sense of the eternal in our transient age, the rectory and all it stands for support us in that endeavour. Within its walls the creative life takes on sacramental importance.

Looks like will contain high poetry but any in to by

CHAPTER ONE

Irregular Regularities

Sydney Smith at Foston

T
HE REVD SYDNEY SMITH (1771–1845), wit, essayist and co-founder of
the *Edinburgh Review*, thrived in metropolitan society. He was never
happier than when he was at his favoured haunts circumscribed by
London's Oxford Street, Piccadilly, Regent Street and Hyde Park, an area he
referred to as 'the great parallelogram'. His innate humour and urbane wit
made him a popular guest and entertaining dinner companion at the tables of
the rich and powerful, in particular in the gracious surroundings of Holland
House in Kensington, home of the Whig hostess Lady Holland. Two hundred
years later his wry pronouncements such as 'I never read a book before
reviewing it; it prejudices a man so', still resonate. He was held in such esteem
– Queen Victoria and Abraham Lincoln were said to be among his admirers –
that Macaulay dubbed him the 'Smith of Smiths'.

However, Smith's sociable and cultured exterior served a more serious
purpose than mere enjoyment. Wit was this impoverished cleric's route to
preferment. Without family money or connections Smith relied on patronage
for advancement in the Church of England, where powerful political patrons
owned the advowsons of many of the increasingly wealthy benefices. But his
Whiggish politics did little to endear him to the Tory political establishment so
it was not until a change of government in 1806, and after much petitioning
from the forceful Lady Holland, that Lord Erskine, the Lord Chancellor, offered
Smith the country living of Foston-le-Clay in Yorkshire, situated between York
and Malton.

Smith commented with some despair on the remoteness of this posting – it was, he said, 'twelve miles from a lemon' – but for three years his London life was largely unaffected by it, as an Act of Parliament passed in 1803, which required priests to live in or near their parishes, was not yet being enforced. Smith employed a curate at Foston for the first years of his incumbency, citing his duties as preacher at Coram's Foundling Hospital in London as a compelling reason for his absence. But in 1809 the recently installed reforming Archbishop of York, Edward Vernon, insisted that residency now be respected both in spirit and to the letter. Smith was obliged to transport himself and his growing family north. He described his predicament:

> A diner-out, a wit, and a popular preacher, I was suddenly caught up by the Archbishop of York, and transported to my living in Yorkshire, where there had not been a resident clergyman for a hundred and fifty years. Fresh from London, not knowing a turnip from a carrot, I was compelled to farm three hundred acres, and without capital to build a parsonage-house.

While some clerical homes grandly declared the social status of their incumbents (and by association the position of the Church of England), the one at Foston was little short of a hovel, consisting of a brick-floored kitchen with one room above it. This situation was not unique. Widespread plurality (clergy holding multiple benefices) meant that parishes frequently had no resident priest. The dilapidated state of many churches and parsonages bore witness to this neglect. The rotting rectory was fast becoming a symbol of the eroded position of the Church of England and its ministers within the rural community. Since the incumbent not only dispensed spiritual guidance but also often had a role in local government as a magistrate, absentee rectors left a social and political vacuum that a succession of lowly curates could not fill. The calibre of the 'galloping curates' racing around the countryside to take as many services as possible (they were paid by the number) was low. In East Grinstead in Sussex in the early nineteenth century there were so many dark-coated curates lodging at the inn on the Horsham road that it became known as the 'Rookery', a term associated with a house of low morals. Without the ties (and tithes) to the land and community of the parish, the clerics and the Church they represented were in danger of becoming disassociated from their congregations.

At first, Smith settled with his entourage – his wife, three young children (a fourth would be born in 1813) and servants – twelve miles away in Heslington, just outside York, riding to his parish every week to take Sunday service. Smith considered his position: 'I am totally neglecting my parish. I *ought* to build,' he wrote to a friend, but he felt uneasy to 'brick down' so much of his money. In 1812, however, with his customary optimism and vigour, he set about building a new rectory. Owing to financial constraints, it could not be a very elaborate affair, but nonetheless the total cost of the works was £4,000. With no family money behind him he was forced to borrow from Queen Anne's Bounty, the fund established to help impecunious ministers finance such a build. The £130 he needed from the living's annual income of £600 to repay his loan would, he declared, keep him 'a very poor man, a close prisoner here for my life'.

He commissioned a local architect, Peter Atkinson, assistant to John Carr of York, to draw up plans. Atkinson came up with a proposal that was prohibitively grand and expensive. Sydney dismissed him with £25 and the admonition, 'You build for glory, Sir; I, for use.' He then sat down in his 'thinking-chair' and together with his ever supportive and loving wife, Catherine, set about drawing up plans for what he would describe as 'the model of parsonage-houses'.

Every day he rode from Heslington on his horse Peter the Cruel to supervise the building works. He acted as architect and foreman, trying to minimize costs where he could. He even experimented with producing his own bricks, but after 150,000 had been ruined in the kiln he decided it would be better to buy the materials and the necessary oxen to pull the carts up to the site. Named Tug and Lug, Hawl and Crawl, the oxen were not a success. The latter pair found the muddy tracks too difficult to negotiate and Tug and Lug 'kept fainting and had to be revived with sal volatile'. Smith was eventually forced to concede: 'I did as I ought to have done at first, – took the advice of the farmer instead of the gentleman; sold my oxen [and] bought a team of horses.'

Smith's boundless energy and personal involvement – 'I live trowel in hand'; 'My whole soul is filled up by lath and plaster' – kept the project moving, although there was a gap of eight weeks when fierce winter frosts meant no work could be done on the house. Finally, on 20 March 1814, five years after they had come north, the family moved into their new home of rose-coloured local brick, set in the middle of a field. The excitement of their 'March landing' is palpable in his daughter Saba's account:

Northern Elevation

Western Elevation

Southern Elevation

Eastern Elevation.

Elevations of Sydney Smith's rectory at Foston, North Yorkshire.
The building was completed in 1814.

How should I forget it? … Waggon after waggon of furniture poured in every minute; the roads were so cut up that the carriage could not reach the door; and my mother lost her shoe in the mud, which was ankle-deep, whilst bringing her infant up to the house in her arms.

. But oh, the shout of joy as we entered and took possession! … Molly Mills, the milk-woman … grinning with delight in the background. We thought it a palace; yet the drawing-room had no door, the bare plaster walls ran down with wet, the windows were like ground-glass from the moisture which had to be wiped up several times a day by the housemaid. No carpets, no chairs, nothing unpacked; rough men bring in rougher packages at every moment.

Despite the lack of comfort, the first evening in what was soon to become known as the 'Rector's Head' – 'equal to any inn on the North Road' – was a convivial affair: 'At last,' Saba recounted in her memoirs, 'we all sat down to tea, spread by ourselves on a huge package before the drawing-room fire, sitting on boxes round it; and retired to sleep on beds placed upon the floor; – the happiest, merriest, and busiest family in Christendom.' Smith recalled going out with a lantern late at night to meet the last cart from Heslington, which contained the cook and the cat and had got stuck in the mud. He managed to establish the late arrivals in the new rectory just before midnight, 'a feat,' he wrote with some pride, 'taking ignorance, inexperience, and poverty into consideration, requiring I assure you, no small degree of energy.'

The ebullient Smith might have interpreted the incumbency at Foston as a life sentence. Yet with his innate humour and practical application, he resolved to make the most of his incarceration: 'I am very much pleased with my house,' he wrote to a friend. 'I aimed at making it a snug parsonage and I think I have succeeded … After finishing it I would not pay sixpence to alter it.' Two hundred years later, and despite a near catastrophic fire after the Second World War, Foston Rectory still bears the imprint of the humanity and idiosyncratic nature of its clerical architect.

Unsurprisingly for a man of such a sociable disposition, the dining and drawing rooms were focal points of rectory life. Smith recommended 'a bay-window looking upon pleasant objects', since he recognized the importance of a room's aspect and surroundings on mood. As the poet W. H. Auden would later observe in his introduction to *The Selected Writings of Sydney Smith* (1956):

'Mentally, like so many funny men, he had to struggle constantly against melancholia: he found it difficult to get up in the morning, he could not bear dimly lit rooms.' Smith himself explained, 'Persons subject to low spirits should make the rooms in which they live as cheerful as possible; taking care that the paper with which the wall is covered should be of a brilliant, lively colour, hanging up pictures or prints, and covering the chimney-piece with beautiful china ... and the tables near should be strewed with books and pamphlets.' The interior design of Foston put these precepts into practice.

The bright, luminous atmosphere of the drawing room was captured by a visitor who described the walls as being of 'the colour you covet, the genuine chromium, with a sort of yellow flowering pattern. It is exquisitely filled with irregular regularities, – tables, books, chairs, Indian wardrobes; everything finished in thorough taste, without the slightest reference to smartness or useless finery.'

The Indian relics were left to Mrs Smith by her mother, although most had been sold to support the family's modest income. The rest of the simple furniture was supplied by Jack Robinson, the carpenter Saba described as having a 'face like a full-moon' whom Smith took into service, establishing him in the barn at Foston with the simple command: 'Jack, furnish my house.' Jack also doubled as serving-man when the occasion demanded.

Unusually for the period, there were no cornices in the rectory at Foston as they were too expensive. Instead, a paper border was pasted onto the ceiling with a line of shade under it that Saba felt 'relieved the eye, and atoned for their [the cornices] absence'. The bedrooms were similarly furnished, unembellished and modest. The prohibitive expense of building high walls meant that Foston's bedrooms had coved ceilings occupying part of the roof space and were papered in a style that was all 'airy, gay, cheap and pretty'. One guest counted twenty-eight unframed Piranesi prints of ancient Rome adorning his bedroom walls. Smith favoured prints hung in this way out of a need for financial restraint as well as a preference for pared-down simplicity.

Likewise, marble chimneypieces were too 'dear', so Smith decided on 'cheap, warm-looking Portland stone' and had it cut according to his own specifications. He also designed the firebacks, which proved so effective – 'I am notorious also for having the warmest house in this part of Yorkshire' – that the society hostess Lady Grey had them copied. As ever at Foston, where architectural detail often had a moral purpose, a brightly burning fire in as many

Foston Rectory. Despite a near catastrophic fire in the 1960s,
Smith's original design is still discernible.

Sydney Smith by Sir Edwin Landseer. As a result of his innovative design for firebacks, Smith was well known for having the warmest house in his part of Yorkshire.

rooms as possible and affordable not only kept the house warm, but also lifted the spirits and, along with the cheery colours on the walls, formed part of Smith's nineteen-point armoury against low moments.

When Smith had lived in Edinburgh as tutor to Michael Hicks Beach he had studied the inventor Count Rumford's descriptions of his experiments, and as an alternative to Rumford's improved fireplace he devised his own 'shadrachs'. These tubes brought air directly from the outside into the centre of his fireplaces, making them burn more brightly. He also secured his poker, tongs and shovel to the wall, preventing them 'from falling with that horrid crash which is so destructive to the nerves', as one grateful guest noted.

Smith liked to read and write amid the bustle of domestic life. So his study was not his retreat, like those of many of his contemporaries, but rather a room 'of less consequence', according to one visitor. It was here that he kept his 'rheumatic armour', an ingenious device consisting of two 'jack-boots; round the throat a hollow tin collar; over each shoulder a large tin thing like a shoulder of mutton; on his head a hollow tin helmet, all filled with hot water.' This patent armour was to be worn around the neck if it was stiff or the patient were suffering from 'a swelled face'. The 'stomach-tin' was the 'greatest comfort in life', aside from 'the tin-slipper', a precursor of the hot-water bottle as a warming device for cold toes, 'which you can sit with in the drawing-room, should you come in chilled, without wetting your feet'. His experiment with making candle-wax out of sheep fat was less successful: he had not accounted for the smell of burning mutton invading every corner of the house.

Smith took an interest in the smallest decorative detail. He disliked large white blinds on the windows – too monastic – and, as he could not afford to pay for painted ones, he suggested his wife and daughters make a patchwork alternative: 'Get rich glazed cottons, combine your colours well, and select a classical pattern, and I am sure the effect will be very good.' As ever, Saba recalls that his inventiveness drew general praise and his 'Foston blinds excited universal admiration'.

The family was happily established in the new rectory, but it had been a labour of love and had involved a large financial investment. Lack of funds meant Smith had to be inventive when establishing his domestic household. Entertaining society friends was his lifeblood – all the more so in exile in rural Yorkshire – and the requirements of form would be adhered to, albeit in his own unique style. Unable to afford a manservant, with typical practical

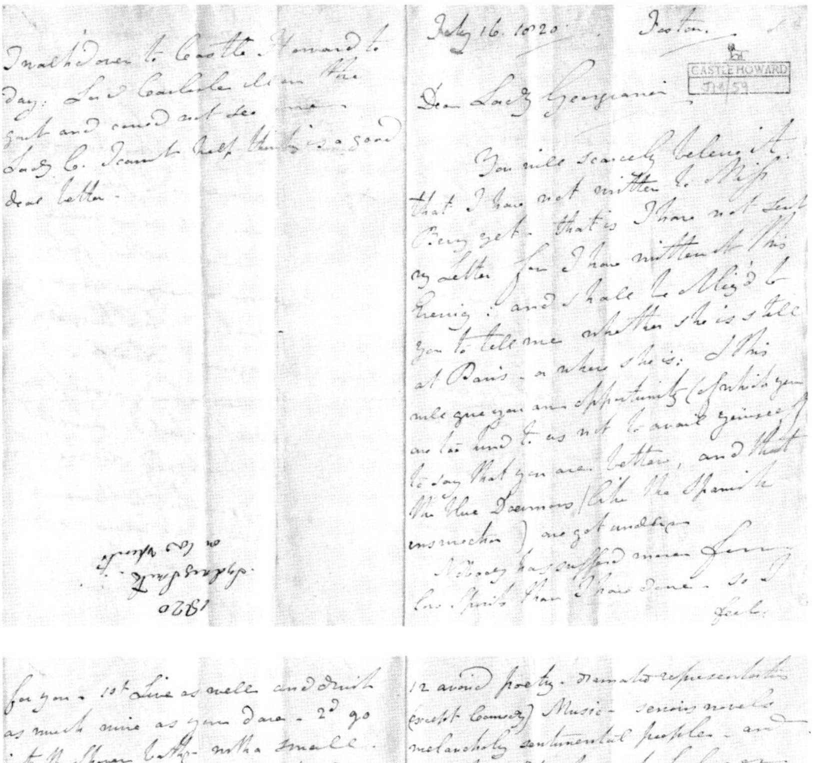
Feby 16. 1820. Foston.

CASTLE HOWARD J18/59

Dear Lady Georgiana

You will scarcely believe it that I have not written to Miss Berry yet. that is I have not sent my letter for I have written it this Evening; and shall to Miss B to you to tell me whether she is still at Paris – or where she is; This will give you an opportunity (of which you are too kind to us not to avail yourself) to say that you are better, and that the blue Daemons (like the Spanish insurrection) are got under.

Nobody has suffered more from low Spirits than I have done – so I feel for you. 1st Live as well and drink as much wine as you dare – 2d go into the Shower bath with a small quantity of water at a temperature low enough to give you a slight sensation of cold – 75 or 80. – 3d amusing books. 4th short views of human life not further than dinner or Tea – 5th be as busy as you can – 6th see as much as you can of those friends who respect & like you – 7th and of those acquaintance who amuse you – 8th make no secret of low Spirits to your friends but talk of them freely – they are always worse for dignified Concealment – 9 attend to the effect Tea and Coffee produce upon you – 10. Compare your lot with that of other people. – 11. dont expect too much from human life, a sorry business at the best. 12 avoid poetry, dramatic representation (except Comedy) Music – serious novels melancholy sentimental people – and every thing likely to excite feeling or emotion – not ending in active benevolence 13 – do good. endeavour to please every body of every degree. 14. be as much as you can in the open air without fatigue 15. make the room where you commonly sit gay & pleasant. 16 Struggle by little and little against idleness – 17. dont be too severe upon yourself, or underrate yourself – but do yourself Justice – 18. keep good blazing fires 19. be firm and constant in the exercise of rational religion. 20. believe me dear Lady Georgiana very truly yrs

Sydney Smith.

I walk over to Castle Howard to day. Lord Carlisle ill in the gout and cannot see me. Lady C. I cannot help thinking is a good deal better.

Sydney Smith on low spirits 1820

Letter from Sydney Smith to Lady Georgiana Morpeth outlining his nineteen-point plan against low spirits, 16 February 1820.

application Smith set about training an existing employee, a 'garden-girl' called Bunch, to become 'the best butler in the county'. Out of doors reigned Molly Mills, who had started as milk-woman and was trained by Smith to add cow-pig-poultry-garden-and-post-woman to her areas of responsibility. Like her master, Molly was renowned in the village for her wit, and 'with her short, red petticoat, her legs like mill posts, her high cheekbones red and shrivelled like winter apples; ... she delighted in a crack with her master, when she could get it.'

The status of the rector also required him to keep a carriage. As a new one was beyond his means, Smith found an ancient green chariot in a coachmaker's yard. With the help of the villagers, he lined and repaired it, and with such annual adjustments and improvements the carriage seemed to grow younger each year, so he christened it 'The Immortal'. Its appearance was greeted with cheers from the local boys and barks from the village dogs. Carriage horses being too expensive, 'The Immortal' was pulled by one of the carthorses drafted in from field work. Clerical dignity, in Smith's inimitable fashion, was maintained. For longer journeys, Smith travelled by stagecoach and was a voluble companion. 'Most people sulk in stagecoaches,' he commented, 'I always talk'; a trait not always to the liking of his companions.

The sheer force of Smith's personality was as evident inside the rectory as out. He thought it one of the greatest luxuries of his life to keep his wife and children laughing for two or three hours every day. The jollity was shared below stairs as well, as one visitor, his friend and co-founder of the *Edinburgh Review* Henry Brougham, later recalled: 'I have seen him at Foston ... drive the servants from the room with the tears running down their faces, in peals of inextinguishable laughter.'

Everything was done in a spirit of fun and eccentricity but this did not preclude a serious mind. 'Do not assume that because I am frivolous I am shallow,' Smith observed wryly to an over-serious dinner companion; 'I do not assume that because you are grave you are profound.' He had drawn huge fashionable crowds to his sermons in London, but was quick to adjust to the requirements of a more humble audience at Foston. He opted for a simple and energetic presentation of basic moral teachings, to which he added his own dramatic flourishes: 'When I began to thump the cushion of my pulpit on first coming to Foston, as is my wont when I preach, the accumulated dust of a hundred and fifty years made such a cloud that for some minutes I lost sight of my congregation.'

With 'a new wheel, a new spring' and the help of his loyal parishioners, Smith transformed a decaying chariot into an idiosyncratic rector's carriage and named it 'The Immortal'.

Smith had arrived at Foston a writer and thinker, not a countryman or farmer. He did shoot, but without much success or enthusiasm: 'When I take a gun in my hand, I am sure the safest place for a pheasant is just opposite the muzzle.' There was also a more serious objection, although as ever he couches it in comical terms: 'if you do shoot, the squire and the poacher both consider you as their natural enemy, and I thought it more clerical to be at peace with both.' He objected to his fellow clergy spending a great deal of time hunting and shooting, regarding such pastimes as a distraction from parochial duties. They also divided the pastor from his flock as sporting clergy were by implication aligned with the squire and the establishment, since only those classes were allowed to shoot. The ordinary working man had to resort to poaching and risk the penalties of the draconian game laws.

'If anything ever endangers the Church,' Smith wrote, 'it will be the strong propensity to shooting for which the clergy are remarkable.' He abhorred the game laws and was reluctant to dole out punishment to those pitiful poachers who came before him in his role as Justice of the Peace. The local magistrates sat in session once a fortnight at an inn called the Lobster House, and many a Foston lad would appear and receive what became known locally as 'a little of Mr Smith's lobster-sauce'.

Smith felt an instinctive sympathy with the poacher against the landowner: 'for every ten pheasants which fluttered in the wood, one English peasant was rotting in gaol,' he wrote. This he knew from personal experience, having accompanied the prison reformer Elizabeth Fry on a visit to Newgate Gaol, where he had seen the horrific conditions in which prisoners were held. Later in his incumbency, he shared with Sir Robert Peel, social reformer and Tory prime minister, a frustration at the increased level of criminalization and lack of space for the growing number of inmates, noting in his correspondence: 'The real truth is the number of convicts is too overwhelming for the means of proven and effective punishment.' He sought to protect his own parishioners from such a fate, refusing to sentence minors, preferring instead to threaten them with 'his own private gallows'. (No such thing existed, of course, but the ruse was usually an effective deterrent.)

Smith's father had been an itinerant merchant and adventurer, never resident in one place long enough to establish himself as a member of the landed gentry, so Sydney had no training in field sports. His antipathy to hunting put him outside the norm for an educated cleric, many of whom felt it their right,

Sydney Smith. His wit masked a profound humanity: 'It is the greatest of all mistakes to do nothing because you can only do a little. Do what you can!'

if not their social duty, to take part in the pastime. Smith had preached an early sermon against the 'sporting clergy of Malton', asking the congregation: 'Is a minister of God to lead the life of a gamekeeper, or a groom?' It was not well received.

With neither the passion nor the seat for hunting, Smith's mount reflected his lack of equestrian prowess. Named Calamity, this Foston-bred horse was a large-boned sluggish creature 'with famine written in his face' who had to be urged on by Smith suspending a small sieve of corn in front of his nose. Calamity threw his master so many times that in the end Smith 'left off riding, for the good of my parish and the peace of my family, for, somehow or other, my horse and I had a habit of parting company'.

As by law he could not let his land and was not a born agriculturalist, Smith realized he needed the advice of his parishioners if he was to succeed in farming his three hundred acres. Although the Church was beginning to distance itself from its agrarian ties, with a bishop in a Parliamentary debate of the time denouncing clergymen wielding 'the scythe and the sickle', Smith invited the local farmers and, unusually, their wives to dine at the rectory, happy to acknowledge their superior wisdom on working the land and keen to learn. To their received knowledge he added his own brand of Smithian farming practice, comically recounted for the readers of the *Farmer's Magazine*. He set up a speaking trumpet in order to issue instructions from the door of the rectory and looked through a telescope to check that his wishes were being carried out. This was a particularly useful method of working as he was not fond of exercise and, with his love of good food and convivial company, he was becoming increasingly rotund.

Through his sheer geniality, Smith broke down any antipathy between farmers and clergy within the parish while improving his knowledge of local rural practices. He recognized how important diet was in maintaining the health of the community and was in the tradition of the poet-rector George Herbert, who had declared in his manual *The Country Parson*, written two hundred years earlier in his rectory at Bemerton, near Salisbury, that a functioning digestive system was vital for a healthy body and soul. To encourage the inclusion of vegetables in the average parishioner's diet, and to help recompense them for the loss of common land through enclosure, Smith divided up three acres of his glebe into sixteenths to be distributed among his parishioners to grow fruit and vegetables or to keep livestock. This glebeland is still recognized today in the village plots known as 'Sydney's Orchards'.

The link between diet and poor health was proved when the harvest failed in 1816. The Smiths, like their parishioners, were forced to eat their own sprouted wheat and lived for a year on 'thin, un-leavened, sweet-tasting cakes, like frost-bitten potatoes, baked on tins, the only way of using this damaged flour'. Such undernourishment was devastating and a dangerous fever soon took hold in the parish: 'Three people died of it and I believe fully sixteen were ill of it,' Mrs Smith remembered. 'Sydney visited them all constantly every day … The poor entirely confided their maladies to him. And he had the satisfaction of being to them eminently useful.'

Understanding the need for pragmatic medical intervention, this parson-doctor turned one of his rooms at the rectory into a dispensary. Ranged on the shelves were his inventively named potions: 'Heart's delight, the comfort of all the old women in the village; Rub-a-dub, a capital embrocation; – Dead-stop, settles the matter at once, – Up-with-it-then needs no explanation; and so on.' He even recorded his medical prowess in verse:

I know all drugs, all simples and all pills:
I cure diseases, and I send no bills.
[…] Fell atrophy has fled from Foston's vale,
And health, and peace, and joy and love prevail.

Smith proudly declared the rectory 'the house to be ill in'. Indeed, he considered it a 'delicate compliment when my guests have a slight illness here'.

Apart from the health benefits, Smith felt the height of civilization was a fine dinner and one of his most enduring published writings was a rhyming recipe for salad dressing, which became particularly popular in America in the nineteenth century:

Two boiled potatoes strained through a kitchen sieve,
Softness and smoothness to the salad give;
Of mordant mustard take a single spoon,
Distrust the condiment that bites too soon!

As bon viveur, gourmand and charismatic host, Smith believed that 'Life is to be fortified by many friendships' and that 'To love, and to be loved, is the greatest happiness of existence.' The convivial atmosphere of the Rector's Head was a magnet for friends journeying north. Marianne, Charles Darwin's sister, visited while she was staying at York and her aunt, Mrs Josiah Wedgwood, wrote afterwards of four of the 'merriest days I ever spent', echoing Brougham's description of the resounding laughter. She continued:

> They have built a very pretty Parsonage, and furnished it very comfortably, without being expensive. I never saw such a manager as Mrs Smith. Everything is so well done without bustle that I can't think how she contrives it. They have a large farm, which he says he manages better than any farmer in Yorkshire; the effect of it is however an air of plenty in every department that is very agreeable ... They see a great deal of company, and in the most agreeable way of friends coming from a distance to spend some days, and not stiff dinner visits.

It is Sydney Smith's force of personality and sheer amiability that suffuse descriptions of life at Foston Rectory. As the practical and spiritual centre of family as well as parish life, his occasional absences to London for necessary business were keenly felt. 'A family doesn't prosper, I see, without a papa!' Saba exclaimed in a letter to a friend. But the merriment at Foston was coming to an end: the award of the living at Combe Florey in Somerset in 1829 brought the family south and in April that year Smith's son Douglas died at the age of 24. Smith wrote about it in his notebook some months later: 'So ends this year of my life – a year of sorrow, from the loss of my beloved son Douglas – the first great misfortune of my life, and one which I shall never forget.' The grieving Smith welcomed the opportunity to distract himself in new surroundings. In the tiny hamlet he found 'a most parsonic parsonage, like those described in novels', although he still took to remodelling it to his own taste, adding a library and introducing his eccentric brand of farming to his glebe.

His tenure at Combe Florey, a parish that in the twentieth century would house the playwright Terence Rattigan and that gentleman rector *manqué*, the novelist Evelyn Waugh, was combined with prebendary duties at Bristol Cathedral. Smith was advancing, but slowly, and the bishopric that he hoped for continued to elude him. Meanwhile, he immersed himself in Somerset life, in his correspondence, in entertaining his many friends and doctoring his parish. He also pushed for social reform, delivering speeches in favour of the Reform Bill of 1832 and writing papers promoting the education of women. His

An Evening Entertainment, *c*. 1804, by John Harden. 'What would you not have given to have heard the mass of wit, sense, anecdote and instruction that flowed incessantly!' wrote one Foston visitor.

Lord and Lady Holland, Dr Allen and William Doggett in the Library at Holland House, 1838,
by C. R. Leslie. Towards the end of his life Smith returned to London to take up his place in
the fashionable salons of the capital. Lord Holland was a relative of Sydney Smith's by marriage
and Chancellor of the Duchy of Lancaster in the period 1830–40.

much-loved daughter Saba, whom he had educated, and who was his right hand in his medical work, married Queen Victoria's physician-in-ordinary Henry Holland in 1834, reputedly having met him in the rectory's dispensary.

Although he never gained the mitre he coveted, Smith's earnings were considerably enhanced when he became a canon of St Paul's in 1831. With an annual income of almost £2,900, he was nearing the top of the clerical ladder. He now divided his time between Combe Florey and London, where he took up his position at the social and fashionable heart of the city that he had left over twenty years earlier. Smith was much in demand as a dinner companion, was elected to The Club, which had been founded by Samuel Johnson and David Garrick, and mixed easily with the literary figures of the day, including the young Charles Dickens. He was also a doting grandfather, entertaining his grandchildren with inventive games in the library at Combe Florey each Christmas.

In July 1844 Smith summed up his life in a letter to a French correspondent: 'I am, upon the whole, a happy man, have found the world an entertaining world, and am thankful to Providence for the part allotted to me in it.' Three months later the ebullient and overweight Smith suffered a serious heart attack in the rectory at Combe Florey and was brought up to London where his physician son-in-law could attend to him. He died in February 1845 and was buried next to his son Douglas in Kensal Green Cemetery.

CHAPTER TWO

Turning Chaos
into Cosmos

Alfred Tennyson at Somersby

T HE VERY WORD SOMERSBY conjures up the image of an English Arcadia
and the landscape surrounding the village on the Lincolnshire Wolds
remains largely unchanged since 1808 when the Revd George Tennyson
and his young wife and growing family made the local rectory their home.
There were to be twelve children (the eldest dying in infancy) born between
1806 and 1819, the most famous of whom was Alfred (1809–92), later Lord
Tennyson, Poet Laureate and the greatest literary celebrity of his age. The
nearest town is Spilsby, six miles away, and even today there is a strong sense of
isolation and otherworldliness in this remote hamlet. There is no village shop,
no pub, and many of the locals do not drive. 'We really live in a different world
from most people,' a contemporary owner of Somersby House, the former
rectory, has remarked.

The vision of a lyrical landscape was captured by Alfred Tennyson's son
Hallam in his biography of his father. Somersby is described as a 'pastoral hamlet'
embosomed in trees, 'in a land of quiet villages, large fields, gray hillsides and
noble tall-towered churches'. Alfred himself wrote of Somersby as being 'secluded
under a chalk-hill, called in the dialect of this county, a wold – a village shadowed
by tall elm trees, with here and there a sand-rock jutting out of the soil'. In high
summer it was lush and green with vegetation, in winter it was bleak and lashed
by winds from the North Sea. Today, Somersby House sits in a deep lane facing
the road, a fine looking white-walled Georgian building with a Gothic hall
attached and an extensive garden stretching away from the back of the house.

Somersby, by Edward Hull. The village on the Lincolnshire Wolds was the subject of many sentimentalized descriptions by Victorian biographers of Tennyson.

Somersby House, formerly the rectory. The Gothic hall on the right was added by
the Revd Dr George Tennyson in 1819 to accommodate his large family.

At first sight the former rectory conveys to the onlooker a sense of quietude, a fitting breeding ground for poetic sensibilities. Hallam recorded his father's memory of the storybook setting: 'He always spoke of it with an affectionate remembrance; of the woodbine that climbed the bay window of his nursery; of the Gothic vaulted dining room with stained-glass windows … making "butterfly" souls on the walls.' This description suggests an entirely appropriate setting for a poet laureate's childhood – the handsome English rectory standing opposite the churchyard, flanked by ancient yew trees with a brook running by.

Alfred, in Hallam's account, gave the impression of a childhood at Somersby spent in the cloistered calm of clerical life. This was only part of the story, however. The myth of pastoral romance, engineered by the Tennyson family in their lifetime and much expanded since, conceals a darker, far more complex truth. Away from the gaze of the parish, life for the Tennyson brood could be intense and, subject to the Revd Tennyson's furious outbursts and mental instability, increasingly fraught as he descended into depression, alcoholism and frequent disturbing bouts of epilepsy. There were violent phases when the children feared for their own and their mother's safety. During a particularly heated argument with his eldest son, a loaded gun had to be wrestled from the rector. The children were forced to retreat from these rages, taking refuge in the attic spaces and the comparative safety of their imaginary worlds. The sketchbooks they filled with drawings and poems in this period reveal the depths of their misery. This strange and difficult childhood would bedevil the family members for the rest of their lives.

The internal contradictions of the Tennysons' life at Somersby are mirrored in the external disjunction of the rectory itself. Bolted onto the solid Georgian façade, the Gothic addition, built by the Revd Tennyson in 1819 to accommodate his large family, still sits a little uncomfortably next to the rather less imposing original structure.

Like his near contemporary, Sydney Smith, George had not envisaged life in a small country rectory. As the elder son of an ambitious and prosperous lawyer, he had been brought up to expect a life of greater freedom and ease. In this he was to be horribly disappointed. In 1790, his father, George the elder, known locally as the Old Man of the Wolds, negotiated for the acquisition of several livings in the county. He was a pragmatic lawyer and businessman and viewed the Church as a suitable career path for the son who would not inherit. His portrait shows him with a hint of smugness around the mouth, but the apparent self-satisfaction masked a depressive and ungovernable tendency. When the Old Man's wife died he declared that 'being unhappy in myself, I make all around me if not miserable, quiet and grave.'

Mystery surrounds the exact circumstances and timing, but George, despite being the elder son, was disinherited in favour of his younger brother Charles. Perhaps the 'black blood' of the Tennysons (now generally accepted as epilepsy) had manifested itself early in George's childhood. Even his mother had described him as 'rude and ungovernable' when a young boy and as a student he showed signs of eccentric behaviour, allegedly firing a shot through a window at Trinity College, Cambridge. In 1801 he embarked on a legendary and improbable journey to Russia, which included insulting a count at dinner in St Petersburg, fleeing from the ensuing duel and spending months lost in penniless wandering before being nursed through weeks of delirium in a village hut in the Crimea.

Whatever the basis in truth of the Russian escapade, the confined existence awaiting George (when he eventually managed to get home on a packet boat) must have seemed like a life sentence. Ordained a priest on 19 December 1802, he was made Rector of Benniworth on 21 December 1806, and ten days later was installed as Rector of Somersby and Bag Enderby, twelve miles to the south on the Lincolnshire Wolds. His aptitude for such a career had never been a consideration. The proximity of all that should have been his at the family estate at Bayons Manor, a mere sixteen miles away in Tealby, must have eaten away at him like a canker. His one consolation was his beautiful wife, Elizabeth Fytche, the daughter of a vicar and niece of the Bishop of Lincoln, whom he had married in 1805. Together they made a striking pair: he tall, dark-haired, with a sallow complexion like all the Tennysons and she, petite and fair, with merry brown eyes and a relaxed manner.

George Tennyson considered the proposed rectory accommodation at Somersby quite inadequate for his household, which, as well as his wife, now comprised their baby son, one manservant and three other servants. Even a disinherited Tennyson required a home declaring a degree of social status and this was not it. Slighted and dissatisfied, he wrote to his father on 24 July 1807 requesting further funds, his bitterness and disappointment spilling out onto the page:

The house was in so miserable a state that I have been obliged to take down the Ceilings of the whole house above & below, except of two rooms. This together with the enlarging of the Kitchen which was only ten feet wide, the building a Nursery over it & two Servants' Rooms above the Nursery without which I should not have had room even for my own family … [and] the number of places to build besides … will cost more than the £120 which I supposed would have covered the Expense … Had I indeed known all the disagreeable circumstances connected with the livings I never could have been induced to accept them.

The shock of finding the rectory in such a state of disrepair was considerable. Nonetheless, it did present the new incumbent with the opportunity to employ his architectural and drafting skills. George's notebooks are full of diagrams and mathematical calculations for the new additions. No detail was left to chance; he calculated everything down to the last brick. Here was a man who combined meticulous attention to detail with a deep fascination with the aesthetic, an interest perhaps too worldly and varied for an incoming parish priest in such a remote hamlet.

At first, George, or Dr George as the locals often referred to him once he had been awarded a doctorate in 1813, seems to have applied himself dutifully to the tasks of running a rural parish. His early notebooks and correspondence reveal his attempts to impose order: sermons are carefully researched and written, annotated with the dates they were delivered and to which congregation. Parishioners' names, ages, type of work (if any) and an estimate of the number of children are dutifully listed, together with calculations of acreage and rents. There are also lengthy treatises illustrated with meticulous diagrams on subjects as diverse as bookbinding and the art of mixing paint colours of his own composition, such as ivory black and profusion blue.

His artistic eye is also evidenced in his detailed lists of the Renaissance schools of drawing and in his treatise on painting draperies, backgrounds and landscapes. His was a mind stimulated by interests outside the parochial. The notebooks contain sketches and quotations that struck him as apposite. This was the time of the Grand Tour, when young men of his background travelled through Europe soaking up the beauty and achievements of Classical Antiquity and the Renaissance. George's Grand Tour was limited to a tour of the imagination, garnering from books what his contemporaries, including his younger brother, experienced first hand. His reality was rooted in the poorer conditions of rural England and his notebooks reveal his attempts to harness the beauties of the Renaissance to his life as a parochial parish priest.

Landlocked in the rectory, deprived of worldly stimulation, George became troubled: 'I am mad Tom and I know it,' he wrote in his notebook. He had no calling for the Church and his sermons burn with an intense struggle between worldly and spiritual emotion: 'Dare we ascribe to the Almighty those disgraceful feelings which corrode and agitate the human bosom? The irascible and revengeful passions arise in the human breast from a various collision of interests, from the offer of some real or imaginary insult, the violation of some right.' The language is urgent and angry, suggesting his own 'irascible and revengeful passions' and the effort to keep them under control. One can only imagine the reaction of his parishioners – mostly agricultural labourers – to his declamations from the pulpit in the little church of St Margaret's. It must have been quite a sight: the imposing, booming-voiced rector addressing his tiny congregation in language unintelligible to them. He would take snuff in the pulpit, play nervously with his hands, and unlike Sydney Smith he seemed incapable of tailoring his themes to the concerns of his audience. As one parishioner later put it, with great economy: ''E read 'em from a paaper and I didn't know what 'e meant.'

Almost every year brought a new birth at the rectory: after Frederick, who was a baby when they arrived, came Charles, Alfred, Mary, Emily, Edward, Arthur, Septimus, Matilda, Cecilia and Horatio. Alfred was born on 6 August 1809. The room of his birth is now boarded up, but Victorian engravings depict it as a simple yet elegant space complete with tester bed and a large sash window looking out onto the garden, an apt birthplace for 'one on whom the Muses had conferred their rarest gifts', as one Victorian admirer put it.

An attic room, reached by its own staircase, became a combined bedroom-study for the three eldest boys, offering them a form of sanctuary, albeit a cramped one. It was to be a constant throughout their lives at Somersby, a haven, set apart from the domestic chaos below, where they could retreat to the inner world of their imagination. Like so many other rectory children, they found in the recesses of the building itself the opportunity to create alternative realities. This room was where Frederick, Charles and Alfred composed their earliest verse. Tennyson himself described it in his early poem 'O Darling Room' (1832), turning the cramped reality into a poetic idyll:

> O darling room, my heart's delight,
> Dear room, the apple of my sight,
> With thy two couches soft and white,
> There is no room so exquisite,
> No little room so warm and bright,
> Wherein to read, wherein to write.

The early pieces of juvenilia consisted mainly of tales of chivalrous knights and were left under the vegetable serving dishes on the dining-room table to be read out as after-dinner entertainment. While young Arthur was under the table 'trying to find God's legs', Alfred would prowl around it like a caged animal, declaiming his verse in sonorous tones.

Dr George took charge of his offspring's education from an early age. Ever the cultured and learned man, in 1805 he had purchased many of the books from the library of Bennet Langton, a friend of Samuel Johnson's, and this acquisition formed the core of Somersby's extensive collection of some 2,500 books. And so the Tennyson boys were immersed in the classics from a young age. By the time he was 7, and under his father's instruction, Alfred had learned all the *Odes* of Horace. He and his brothers would have to write commentaries on the subtleties of C. G. Heyne's edition of Homer to show that they had read and understood the text. According to Alfred's inscription in the front of his copy of Heyne, 'We followed the same command of his, writing in our Horaces ... the criticisms of several commentators.' Such rigorous standards were not employed in the little Louth grammar school that the older boys later attended and where they learned 'absolutely nothing'. Alfred under-lined these last two words twice.

The boys' precocity was extraordinary but it made them outsiders not only in Somersby but also in the wider world. Despite its demons, the one place where this eccentric family felt they belonged was in their crowded rectory. After five unhappy and unproductive years boarding sixteen miles away at Louth, the boys returned home. Frederick as the eldest was then sent off to Eton where he cut a lonely figure, describing himself as 'a person of gloomy insignificance and unsocial monomania'. He had a special loathing for the aristocracy, complaining of the 'high jinks of the high-nosed who go about with well-cut trousers and ill-arranged ideas'.

Dr George now became even more obsessed with the education of the boys, perhaps as a form of self-redemption, writing to his brother: 'Phoenix-like I trust (though I don't think myself a Phoenix) they will spring from my ashes, in consequence of the exertions I have bestowed upon them.' It was a harsh and demanding regime and a villager remembered Dr George could be 'amazing sharp' with his sons. To escape his temper and increasing despondency, they spent much time outside, either in the kitchen garden that flourished in charming disorder, or in the stream later immortalized in Alfred's famous poem 'The Brook'. There, according to Hallam, Alfred used to 'build cities and castles of sand till the current undermined them and the towers fell' (now regarded as a metaphor for the unstable Tennysons) or despatched little bits of wood 'freighted with imaginary wares for China and India till an eddy overwhelmed them'. More dramatically, Alfred once threw himself on a grave in the church-yard, railing against the heavens and wishing he were dead. Yet he and his brothers clearly admired and loved their father, despite his irascibility and morbidity. '*Ex dono patris amicissimi*' (A gift from a father who is a very good friend), was inscribed in Alfred's copy of Virgil's *Opera*.

It was not only the sons who were educated; unusually for the period, the Tennyson sisters were also voracious readers and occasionally poets, and even formed their own literary society – the Husks. They avoided the accepted domestic pastimes of the sampler and needlepoint – 'nivver could sampler, nor knit, nor sew', one parishioner later recalled, with some bewilderment – and were almost as 'high-larnt as the boys', all of which added to their aura of not being quite fit for conventional society. For the villagers, 'to hev owt to do wi books', whether the boys or the girls, evoked pity as to them it was a sign of weak intellect: '*poor things*! they would allus hev a book i' their hands.'

It was an unusual and somewhat chaotic existence. Mrs Tennyson, exhausted by a near-constant state of pregnancy, seems to have left her children to their own devices, indulging them rather than imposing a disciplined regime. She often forgot to order provisions for the table until they were all seated around it, at which point she had to send urgently to the local farm for a brace of ducks. Notwithstanding, they all adored her. She was frequently seen being pulled about the country lanes in a basket chair by her tall lanky sons, or by a huge Newfoundland dog (with hooves, according to village gossip), which,

Somersby Rectory, *c*.1889, when it was revered as the birthplace of the Poet Laureate.

The Gothic hall of the rectory, depicted in a nineteenth-century engraving.
The Revd Dr George Tennyson designed the addition, including the
carved wooden mantelpiece.

when the weather was hot, would lie down in the road and refuse to proceed until he was rested. On these expeditions Mrs Tennyson would read aloud to her prone offspring (and the dog) from James Thomson's poetry cycle *The Seasons* (1730) or from the works of James Beattie.

Mrs Tennyson's menagerie also included a pet owl, trained by Alfred to sit on her head, and a domesticated monkey whose party trick was to run a lighted candle down his spine. Knowing she was indulgent of animals, local boys used to beat their dogs under her window until they howled in complaint, whereupon she threw down coins so they would stop teasing the poor creatures.

The claustrophobic atmosphere within the rectory walls increased as the children grew. In 1815, with seven children, Dr George was complaining that the ongoing building works at Somersby were using up all his ready money. Downstairs he amalgamated three cramped rooms to give the family the only place in the house where they could gather. By 1819, now with eleven children, yet more space was needed. Together with his ever loyal and equally irritable manservant and coachman Horlins, Dr George planned a substantial addition to accommodate his burgeoning family. This was the Gothic hall, a room where the whole family could meet to dine, sit and converse. Horlins and his master, an unlikely pair, shared a passion for building; Horlins took charge of the brickwork and his master the internal design and decoration, including the intricate wood carving over the mantelpiece and the front door. It was a whimsical, ecclesiastical addition to this idiosyncratic home.

Despite the extra space, the atmosphere inside the rectory became more intense. There was little escape from Dr George's increasing instability, depression and violent mood swings. He brooded more and more on his social and financial inferiority to his brother Charles (whose branch of the family later styled themselves Tennyson-D'Eyncourt, not least to create some distance from their Somersby cousins), and his two sisters, all comfortably off. He could not help dwelling on what he imagined was the ease of their lives and compared their prosperity with his lot in a cramped rectory, deprived of his birthright. Complaining of his wealthier sister's imminent visit, he wrote: 'We are three and twenty in family and sleep five or six in a room. Truly we have great accommodation for Mrs Russell and her suite.'

In 1821, Somersby held seventy-nine parishioners, twenty-three of whom lived in the rectory. Hallam Tennyson would later portray the villagers as 'uncouth and mannerless', though a similar epithet could equally have been used for the inhabitants of the Tennyson home. For all the intellect and learning, it was not an orderly household and their behaviour was often outside the norm. The entire family kept strange hours, wandering the lanes in the middle of the night, and Dr George would sometimes sleep in the afternoon and then wake to play the harp when everyone else was sleeping. The Tennysons, removed from society due to their unusual upbringing, their precocity and the location of the village of Somersby itself, were freed from society's conventions. Personal hygiene, for example, was low down on the list of priorities and the Tennyson malady or 'black blood' often manifested itself in extreme indolence. Their appearance, too, marked them out as different. They were a strikingly good-looking family, their dark colouring distinguishing them from their paler neighbours. It was as if a group of Spaniards had landed in Lincolnshire. Everything about them was unconventional: 'they were never like ordinary people; even their dress and their walk seemed "different".' Nonetheless, the daughter of the rector of Owmby-cum-Searby recalled, perhaps with the naïveté of childhood: 'They might ramble, stalk, saunter or stride over the country-side and be sure of a warm welcome wherever they went, for their genuine friendliness made them universally liked.'

The Tennysons' strangeness seems only to have added to the romantic aura of the family in the locality. Alfred, coming across a party of friends and family in Holywell Wood, fixed Emily Sellwood (who would later become his wife) with his piercing brown eyes, and enquired: 'Are you a Nereid or a Nymph?' In turn, when she first saw him she could not imagine 'anything more beautiful in human form'.

If Alfred was physically beautiful he was also unkempt: a Somersby servant remembered him as 'a 'dacious one. He used to be walking up and down the carriage drive hundreds of times a day shouting and holloaing and preaching, with a book always in his hand and such a lad for making sad work of his clothes … down on his heels and his coat unlaced and his hair anyhow. He was a rough 'un was Mister Halfred and no mistake.' Paradoxically, given their coarse appearance, the brothers were in fact self-conscious about their dress. They favoured long flowing capes and dark sombreros, stylish armour perhaps against the prying eyes of strangers and critics (the Tennyson sensibility found any criticism excessively wounding).

In later life, despite his fame, Alfred was still a fiercely private man. Having grown up in a household with its own hidden demons, he railed against those

Alfred Tennyson as a young man, *c.* 1840. Rosa Baring from neighbouring Harrington Hall
remembered the local girls feeling 'as proud as peacocks to have been
worthy of notice by him'.

who wanted to reveal the intimate details of the lives of public figures. When unflattering memories of Dr Johnson were published, Alfred took a robust stance: 'If one knew all one would pardon all, is much more likely to be the truth,' he declared, and 'The poet's work is his life, and no one has a right to ask for more.'

This sensitivity to the tension between the public and private was rooted in his experience of life at Somersby. The dislocation between what was expected in public and what was going on inside the rectory pushed the entire Tennyson family to the edge of reason during the 1820s. It was a Somersby legacy that would remain with them – only three of the children (including Alfred) avoided being institutionalized at some stage of their life. For Dr George the strain of attempting to be a good parish priest and father while his whole being rebelled against the life that had been forced upon him was too much. By the time he was 40, in 1818, he suffered severely from depression, alcoholism and savage seizures.

The family feared each attack, believing that it reduced his intellectual powers and left him physically weakened but increasingly violent. His sister Eliza recognized his need to get away from the confines of parish life: 'locomotion is the only thing I believe for spirits like ours when depressed and fixing exclusively on one subject,' she wrote in July 1827. Although George could take occasional excursions from Somersby, and indeed was a convivial and much-favoured guest with many of the county families, there was no escaping his life there or his responsibilities. Trapped in a downward spiral, he was taking his family with him.

By October 1827 a family friend, the Revd William Chaplin, was describing terrible scenes inside the rectory. George had become a mad jailer, deranged through excessive drinking and horrid paroxysms and 'dangerously disposed to his wife and children ... He will not allow the children to go to school, nor even clothe them,' Chaplin reported, adding 'The children are alarmed at him and the wife in the greatest fright both in day and night.' It was no longer possible to conceal the rector's mental state from his parishioners. His fits began to come on in church 'so everyone is afraid of him, and the church neglected' and many of his parish duties were consequently abandoned. Horlins, his faithful servant, was by now the only person who had any influence on him. It was a sordid state of affairs. George refused to pay any household bills, nor would he allow the necessary food for his family.

Witnessing such self-destruction, the Tennyson brood were driven further into their own private worlds. The children's albums from this time are peopled with devilish figures, half-man and half-beast, depicted as 'soaked in baccy and beer'. There are also sketches by the girls of Gothic and romantic castles, and ladies living in gentler worlds than their own. Charles – no doubt to alleviate the misery of what he described as those 'drowsy, hazy, obnubilated, gloomy, wet, blue-devil begetting, sunless, hopeless, joyless days of November' – may have become romantically involved with the girls' music mistress who was deemed an unsuitable match.

The sense of isolation bred at Somersby followed Alfred in 1827 to Trinity College, Cambridge, where, despite making intimate friends, notably Arthur Hallam, the dedicatee of his great poem *In Memoriam*, he remained beset by feelings of loneliness. In the holidays he returned to Somersby where, during Dr George's absences for various cures, there were sunnier, happier times. In 1832 Arthur Hallam visited and spent five weeks there courting Alfred's sister Emily. Sir Charles Tennyson's biography of his grandfather describes an idyllic interlude, with 'much making of music with her and Mary, much reading of poetry in the Rectory drawing-room or on the lawn sloping down to the meadow and the brook, much digging in the garden ... many walks over the wolds and the marsh.' There were dances, too, and visits from other Cambridge and local friends, such as the beautiful local heiress Rosa Baring from Harrington Hall. Yet even during these brief periods of happiness, the Tennysons' otherness set them apart. Alfred was a fine dancer and evidently wonderfully charismatic company when he wanted to be. He was not, however, good enough for Rosa, whose family turned down his suit. There were also lesser, more mundane humiliations for the hypersensitive Alfred, such as the occasion at a dance when his partner's white-gloved hand came away from his shoulder covered in a black sooty substance. A Somersby servant had used boot polish to try and restore some long-lost lustre to Alfred's old evening coat.

As life at Somersby became more extreme, the long-suffering Mrs Tennyson moved out, taking her youngest children with her. Such behaviour in the 1820s was enough to cause a scandal. Dr George was left alone in his rectory, according to his old friend Dr Rawnsley, 'feeding upon himself'. He rallied once more and his wife moved back in but she was soon forced to recall Charles and Alfred from Cambridge as the final stages of George's alcoholism and degradation took hold. There was one last drama when the cook was set on fire in mysterious

A page believed to be from Arthur Tennyson's childhood notebook.

Brothers in Misery, a sketch by one of the Tennyson children.

circumstances and so badly burned that she died three days later. Dr George had reportedly also been seriously injured trying to put out the fire. There was malicious gossip, and villagers then talked of the Tennysons keeping a large vat of water by the kitchen door in case any other servants burst into flames.

Dr George died on 16 March 1831, sitting in a chair in a dingy room downstairs at Somersby. His son Charles wrote: 'his countenance ... was strikingly lofty and peaceful ... which on earth was daily racked by bitter fancies and tossed about by strong troubles.' Without his morose presence, life was calmer. Somersby, however, remained the focus of the unhappy drama that was the Tennyson family's life. One evening in September 1833, Mary and Matilda had seen a tall figure clothed in white move down the lane in front of the rectory. They followed it until it passed through a hedge where there was no gap and disappeared. Matilda was very unnerved by this and two weeks later she had an explanation of the ghostly apparition. On 1 October she was in Spilsby for a dancing lesson and collected a letter from the post office addressed to Alfred. When she returned home to the rectory Matilda found her brother sitting at a table in the dining room; she gave him the letter and went upstairs. It was from Arthur Hallam's uncle, telling Alfred of the untimely death from apoplexy of his greatest friend and Emily's fiancée. Alfred broke the terrible news to Emily. This was a body blow to the family, for whom Hallam had come to represent their hope for the future. That hope had now been extinguished in a tragedy that would be worked and reworked into *In Memoriam*.

A change was forced upon the Tennysons in 1837 when the new rector wanted to take up residence. They left reluctantly; despite being the scene of so much misery, the rectory was the one place where the family felt they belonged. Attempts were made to forge a path in the outside world but somehow the Tennyson temperament and the unique circumstances of their lives at Somersby had made them ill equipped for survival in 'normal' society.

Of the eleven offspring only Charles was ever to have a conventional career. He followed his father into the Church, but also into lengthy battles with alcohol and laudanum. Frederick left the country and wrote sporadically, his best work produced when he returned imaginatively to the domestic detail of the rectory. Horatio was 'rather unused to the planet'; according to a friend who met him in London in 1843, 'one day he was to go to Cheltenham, another to Plymouth: then he waited for an umbrella he thought he had left somewhere. So where he is now I have no notion.'

The Revd Dr George Tennyson, who died in 1831, in a sketch by one of his children.

In Edward this otherworldliness was so extreme that he was placed in a mental asylum in Louth and never released, dying there seventy years later. Charles, too, spent some time institutionalized, as did Arthur who, having taken seriously to drink, was admitted in 1842 for several years to the Crichton Institution in Dumfries, a place that seems to have served as half lunatic asylum and half hospital for the treatment of nervous diseases. Septimus, by his own admission 'the most morbid' of the Tennysons, never escaped the demons of Somersby and died alone and unmarried of a combination of alcohol and extreme inertia, aged 51.

However, the peculiarly sequestered circumstances of Somersby fostered in Alfred a unique poetic talent. The spirit that had been held in check inside the rectory, subsumed to the will of his father, was freed once outside its walls: 'I was in the habit on a stormy day', he later wrote, 'of spreading my arms to the wind and crying out, "I hear a voice that's speaking in the wind," and the words "far, far away" had always a strange charm for me.'

In Alfred, the unhappy Dr George would realize his ambition to have his offspring – in the end only one – rise Phoenix-like from his ashes. Despite the hidden suffering, genius had been nurtured within the walls of Somersby Rectory, although, as Thomas Carlyle observed in 1844, some of the particular Somersby spirit continued to haunt Alfred: 'A man solitary and sad, as certain men are, dwelling in an element of gloom, – carrying a bit of Chaos about him, in short, which he is manufacturing into Cosmos!' In 1832 Alfred achieved public if not critical acclaim with his volume of poems that included 'The Lady of Shalott' and 'The Lotus-Eaters', and ten years later another volume appeared with 'Morte d'Arthur' and 'Locksley Hall'. *In Memoriam* was published in 1850 and its poetic articulation of private grief touched a nation; 60,000 copies were sold in the first six months. In the month following publication, Alfred, after an engagement of twelve years, married Emily Sellwood, the sister of Louisa, wife of his brother Charles. It was a long and happy marriage and signified a new beginning. This miraculous year concluded with his appointment as Poet Laureate, following the death of William Wordsworth, and for the next forty years his was the voice of Victorian poetry.

CHAPTER THREE

An Agreeable Mystery

Dorothy L. Sayers at Bluntisham

T HE TWENTIETH CENTURY was slow to announce itself at Bluntisham-cum-Earith, on the edge of the Fens. Life there continued much as in Anthony Trollope's fictional Framley Parsonage, seemingly untouched by the forces of Victorian doubt, Darwinism and the satirical portrayal of the church hierarchy. Bluntisham, a fine living belonging to Christ Church, Oxford, was worth £1,500 a year in 1897, when it was offered to the Revd Henry Sayers, previously headmaster of Christ Church Choir School, and father to a precociously intelligent only child, Dorothy Leigh Sayers (1893–1957).

Like many rural parishes in the Fenland, Bluntisham-cum-Earith was populated mainly by agricultural labourers of deeply conservative tastes and customs. The novelist and agricultural reformer H. Rider Haggard, in *Rural England* (1902), his report on the impoverishment of the English farming community, could find little to recommend the area: 'Cambridgeshire has but few resident gentlefolk, except, of course, the clergy. In the Fens … hardly anyone will live save those who are actively concerned in the management of the land, since here are to be found neither sport, scenery nor society.' If not a fertile landscape for social stimulation, it was agriculturally productive and the parishioners would not have presented too straitened or demanding a prospect for the high-minded, dutiful Revd Sayers. It was a tempting living because he was not a young man, having come to marriage and fatherhood late, and was tiring of his joint responsibility as headmaster of the choir school and chaplain to the college. He had a notion his monastic and musical tastes would be well suited to the quiet life offered by a comfortable country rectory. His wife, the vivacious and intelligent Helen Sayers, was not so keen.

Helen harboured no illusion about the move from Oxford to an isolated Cambridgeshire parish. When the decision had been taken and her fate sealed, she called the servants together and painted a rather gloomy picture of what lay ahead. The work would be harder and the life much duller without the shops or amusements of Oxford. There was no question of the Revd Sayers's predominantly female entourage not following him, but they did so with heavy hearts. The exodus was later recalled in solemn terms by Dorothy, who was only 4 at the time of the move: 'And so, on this occasion, we went out patriarchally into the wilderness with our manservant and our maidservants and everything that was ours.'

It was not perhaps a wilderness of such biblical proportions ('Like Sherlock Holmes, I never could resist a touch of the dramatic,' Dorothy later confessed), but compared to city living with all its entertainments, the remote village presented an uninspiring prospect to the convivial Helen Sayers. Indeed, she is notably absent from Dorothy's recollection of the all-female party's first sighting of the rectory itself as they were walking up from Bluntisham station,

> my Grandmother in her widow's weeds and my Aunt carrying Polly in a travelling cage. I am walking beside Nurse. I am wearing a brown pelisse and little close bonnet to match, both trimmed with a feathery brown-and-white trimming which must have been a kind of marabout. The time of year is early January, and as we pass in at the gate, I see, for the first time, winter aconites flowering at each side of the drive, from which I conclude that the winter was a mild one.

Dorothy dresses the moment of their arrival as a romantic, dream-like scene, but her account is rescued from sentimentality by sharply observed domestic details, drawn with telling accuracy. The child is centre stage, the first-person narrator. Appropriate deductions made from the visual clues of the winter aconites hint at a young mind already assimilating and interpreting her surroundings. This elegant rectory, sitting in splendid isolation on the edge of the Fens, would be both home and inspiration for one of the greatest writers of the golden age of detective fiction.

Until the seventeenth century, the Fens had been a dark, dank swamp of peat, whose inhabitants were said to be web-footed. The land had then been

The Sayers Family arriving at Bluntisham Rectory, by Norah Lambourne.

reclaimed for agricultural use through a series of complicated drains and dykes. This man-made drainage system is still in use today, keeping the waters of the North Sea at bay. The defences are still occasionally overwhelmed by the force and scale of the water reclaiming its own, such as in 1953, with disastrous consequences for the Fen people and their livelihoods. This natural threat was an ever-present danger for the residents of Bluntisham Rectory and the endless brooding water continued to haunt Dorothy long after she had left. As she wrote in an article in the *Spectator* in 1937:

> Year after year, we could see from our front window the overflowing of the upper Ouse, that turned plough and pasture into standing water … Year by year, Earith parishioners from outlying places excused lateness at church by the natural explanation that the water was over the causey and they had had to wait for the ferry. Year by year, a journey by train in almost any direction found us looking from the carriage-window over a sheet of sullen water, broken only by the lines of sunken hedges and the tops of willow and poplar trees.

Dorothy was to draw on accounts of the 1713 floods in *The Nine Tailors* (1934), the Lord Peter Wimsey mystery set in a fictionalized Bluntisham, where the waters released by a broken sluice gate provide a dramatic finale to the story.

The Sayers family was marooned on its rectory island. Water surrounded them, but ironically it was not so readily available inside the house, where every drop had to be pumped up by hand and carried upstairs in immense brown cans to fill hip-baths. It may have struck the outsider as a grand gentleman's home, but its dignified presence in the parish came at a cost to those gentlefolk confined within its walls.

Bluntisham Rectory is an elegant three-storied building with a square front and ivy-covered wings framed by huge ancient trees that reminded Dorothy of Tennyson's immemorial elms (although in reality they were mainly beech). The house had been refronted in 1848 when Oliver Cromwell's house in nearby St Ives had been pulled down. Cromwell's doorway was transported to Bluntisham and incorporated in the rectory to make an impressive entrance – the last trace of the Lord Protector's home safely reabsorbed back into the Established Church. The initials carved in the overdoor frieze were one of Dorothy's unsolved mysteries of childhood: hours were spent pondering on the meaning of the letters and their design, although any secret they contained remained undeciphered.

Standing in three acres of gardens, the rectory is named in land registers of the early seventeenth century, but it was not until the incumbency of the Revd Samuel Knight a century later that a gentleman's residence emerges. The Revd Knight built 'an excellent house, and laid out a great deal of money in gardens about it', but his attempts at establishing a civilized presence to withstand the wild Fenland weather suffered a literal blow in 1741 when a cataclysmic hurricane untiled the roof and ripped statues and balustrades from their garden settings. It was not until the early 1800s that another incumbent, the Revd Tillard, made a further attempt to tame this wild corner of England and built a new rectory among fine trees and flowerbeds, offering to the traveller on the Ely road an uplifting representation of the comfortable union of Church and State in an otherwise barren landscape. This, with the addition of its dignified new frontage, was the foundation of the fine rector's residence that greeted the Sayers family in January 1898.

If the residence spoke of order and balance, the parishioners themselves did not live in such unadulterated harmony. As in many country parishes in proximity to what had been the Parliamentarian stronghold of Cambridge, there remained a strong Nonconformist presence. These Dissenters were grouped at Earith, at the far western end of the parish. Earith, meaning mud, or gravel, lay unhealthily close to the river and was linked to the more refined Bluntisham by an ancient bridge and causeway – Earith Causey – that had been maintained by hermits until the fifteenth century. This was home to the Quaker population of the parish after 1650, and there is still a meeting house in a deserted spot to the west of the village. A Wesleyan Chapel and a spartan Mission Room complete the Nonconformist patchwork at Earith, the poorer architectural relations of the splendid soaring spire of the thirteenth-century Bluntisham church.

In 'Cat O'Mary', Dorothy's fictionalized account of her childhood (written in 1934 but not published until 2002), the rector's wife expresses the deep mistrust of Dissenters that was still prevalent at the turn of the twentieth century. Their beliefs were feared as a contagion that would spread through the parish like the diptheria that was believed to be carried via the water supply running through the Dissenters' graveyard. The parishioners in *The Nine Tailors* take a similarly dim view of having to toll the bell to mark the passing of

Bluntisham Rectory, one of the finest livings in the gift of Christ Church, Oxford.

The church of St Mary, Bluntisham. Dorothy would later transpose this parish church into *The Nine Tailors*, her Lord Peter Wimsey detective novel set in the Fens.

every Christian soul, 'dissenter and church alike', even, to the horror of old Hezekiah, 'for a Roman'. In reality, Dorothy's own mother, Helen, displayed dissident tendencies herself, albeit concealed within the establishment exterior. She was an independent and progressive thinker who indulged in that most unfeminine of habits (for the time), smoking. She also disapproved wholeheartedly of teetotallers and, fortunately for Dorothy, held distinctly modern views on the education of women. A college place was the aim for her daughter and consequently Dorothy always felt she was destined for Oxford and academe.

The imposing frontage of Bluntisham Rectory befits one of the richest of Christ Church livings. Inside, however, there were numerous quaint and much older rooms, most of which the previous incumbent, the avuncular Canon John Rumpf, had not troubled to keep in good repair during his long residency (1859–97). A single man with unsophisticated taste and surprisingly fruity language for a cleric, Rumpf had trusted to God to provide. He declared that the rectory would last his time, before eventually passing on the burden of dilapidations to the Revd Sayers. The living had been obtained in 1896 by Christ Church in exchange for several smaller parishes, hence the anomaly of an Oxford chaplain being transferred to a living thirteen miles from the university city of Cambridge. Sayers was the first incumbent appointed under this new management, and it fell to the new mistress of the house to ensure that Bluntisham's interior decoration caught up with its gracious façade.

Helen did her best to stop the rot of decay creeping through the house. In this she was aided by a small legacy inherited in the months prior to the 'great change', as Dorothy always referred to their move. This allowed her to redecorate completely the house and provided her with a modicum of independence. Poring anxiously over a great book filled with wallpaper patterns in the months preceding the exodus, Helen made her plans to civilize Bluntisham's interior. A firm of painters and decorators from Oxford was brought in, much to the dismay of the local tradesmen. Such an important task could be entrusted by Helen only to those who belonged to her Oxford life and would therefore understand her requirements.

Helen craved the society and civilization that, for her, were not to be found in a country parish. Oxford was her natural habitat and she would often return there for long visits. A vivacious and attractive woman with an abundance of brown hair, she had a face 'too decided for actual beauty', according to her

The lively and enlightened Helen Sayers, Dorothy's mother, preferred the stimulating life of Oxford to that in a parish backwater.

The hall, Bluntisham Rectory, in a drawing possibly by Dorothy L. Sayers.

daughter, Dorothy, 'but her broad, intelligent forehead, speaking eyes and liveliness of expression' made her much admired. However, she was highly strung and suffered from nervous attacks. The idea of parish duties filled her with horror and although she undertook them as expected, she had no affinity to the country parish or its parishioners, describing their choice of millinery as 'fit only for the local flower show'. She took secret revenge on the teetotallers by lacing the trifles at parish gatherings with generous supplies of sherry.

During Helen's frequent absences, she had a ready replacement in her sister Mabel, who lived with them, and in her mother-in-law, Grannie Sayers, another permanent resident of the rectory and an enthusiastic helper in the parish. As widow of a cleric and mother to two more, she had firm ideas of what was expected and was ever poised to ensure that the parochial mission was performed where needed – even, perhaps, where she was not so needed, or, indeed, welcome.

In Dorothy's autobiographical fragment 'My Edwardian Childhood', she recounts how, for Helen, the rectory was full of draughty cold passages, the hall unwelcoming and the shallow winding staircase 'poor'. But Dorothy remembered the hall as one of the house's most attractive features: 'very long, squareish in the middle and tapering to a narrow passage at either end, through round arches draped with heavy, dark blue-patterned curtains looped up with thick cords and tassles.' The stone floor was covered with brown linoleum (just becoming popular for use in hallways and passages, presumably to maintain the warmth rather than to imitate parquet flooring). The 'poor staircase' also appealed to Dorothy, who found a particular banister 'individual and exciting' as from time to time it oozed a thick, gummy tear of resin. Her mother was, however, right about the cold, which was only partially alleviated by the large Tortoise stove under the staircase. Dorothy liked to be held up to look at the figure of the tortoise on the top and she wondered at the mysterious legend: 'Slow but Sure Combustion'.

Helen was in some ways a disappointed woman. Of exceptional intellect but without the education the male members of her family had received (her solicitor father was also a Latin scholar), the questioning of accepted mores was in her blood (her great-uncle, Percival Leigh, was a famous satirist and early contributor to *Punch*). She was determined that her daughter would receive an education that would equip her for independent living. As a very young child, Dorothy was carried down every morning to the sanctity of her mother's bedroom, where she was read to, avidly following the shape of the words in her mother's book. She could recognize the form of words before she could fully understand them, which led to the odd misapprehension: 'A General Confession', the collective prayer that opens the service of Morning Prayer, was interpreted by the young Dorothy as 'A General Confusion', a stage direction and an entirely apt description of the coughing, shuffling and other distracting noises of the Bluntisham congregation settling down to prayer.

As she grew, Dorothy's books of choice were established as Daniel Defoe's *Robinson Crusoe*, Grimm's *Fairy Tales* and her father's favourite, Joel Chandler Harris's *Uncle Remus*. This was a surprisingly fierce selection for an Edwardian rector's daughter and indicative perhaps of a masculine appetite for bloodthirsty adventure. Dorothy's was a sensibility not fed by the creations often served up by strict nurses to frighten their charges into submission, as her mother had banned from the nursery the use of the popular alarmist tools of bogeymen and hobgoblins. Night-time, therefore, held no fear for Dorothy, who in any case 'was always readily able to distinguish between fact and fiction and to thrill pleasantly with a purely literary horror'. When asked by a cousin if she believed in fairy tales her reply was that she believed these things had happened, 'but a long time ago, and in some quite different place – not this world at all'. Dorothy's world was set apart, safe, ordered, controlled; any dangers threatened by sinister fantasies were firmly located in the realm of fiction and did not impinge on her daily reality. She was not quite so brave physically, rarely venturing beyond the gates of the rectory garden unaccompanied, fearful of illness, unable to swim and terrified of going blind and being unable to read.

It was a structured household, revolving around a strict routine established by her father, the ex-headmaster. All the family members as well as the servants were summoned by the bell at 8.30 a.m. for morning prayers in the dining room. Papered in blue with a meandering pattern and hung with photogravures of seascapes by Peter Graham, with two fluted white pillars supporting a beam at one end, this was the finest room in the house. To the young Dorothy, its expanses were a delight. Much larger than its cramped equivalent at the Sayers's former home, it was an Aladdin's cave with all the ornaments from the Oxford drawing room piled in rich, opulent confusion onto the sideboard, or 'ante-chapel', behind the pillars. These ornaments were an endless source of glamorous imaginings.

The Revd Henry Sayers, Dorothy's father. The tall, bookish, former headmaster of
Christ Church Choir School came to fatherhood late in life.

The Revd Sayers took up his position at the head of the table and waited as the servants filed in to join the family: cook, housemaid, kitchen maid and the only other male member of the household, appropriately referred to in 'Cat O' Mary' as 'The Man ... a kind of house–stable amphibian, [who] appeared in a blue-and-white striped house-coat hastily assumed over his outdoor nether-garments, and was subsequently banished from Christian society on the ground that his boots smelt strongly of horse-manure.' The end of prayers was marked by a strict pause with the rector looking at his watch; breakfast followed in the dining room for the adults and in the nursery for Dorothy, while the servants filed back along the flagstone corridors to the kitchen to continue their day's work.

As an only child set apart from adults in her nursery world, and physically removed from the company of many other children, Dorothy had abundant opportunities for self-dramatization. Yet there is no sense of the self-pity of a loveless or abandoned child in her memoirs, rather the lively drama of a carefully constructed imaginary world with the child-narrator at its centre.

The main protagonists in her nursery dramas were her family of toy monkeys who had accompanied her from Oxford. They enjoyed, sometimes endured, but always survived, endless adventures. Jacko, the eldest, was bald, having been shorn by Dorothy as soon as she could wield a pair of scissors, and had a flat nose, reduced by compulsive sucking ('I can taste the pleasant flavour to this day,' the adult Dorothy remarked). Jacko's glass eyes had been replaced by brown buttons, but he was much loved and the hero of her tales. Jocko was brown and had more fur and a more straightforward character, with less personality than his elder brother. These two were later replaced by Micko and Mocko, but 'they were never such favourites'. The villain of the piece was a rag doll, embroidered in blue and red with a pointed cap and black hair and eyes, named 'Frenchman'. Not exactly loved, but necessary for dramatic purposes.

These companions gave narrative colour to an otherwise uneventful life at the rectory, and they often appeared in her correspondence. Writing to her mother in Oxford in January 1900, Dorothy confides: 'Do you know the little animals confessed to me that *they steal Polly out of the kitchen and ride him*!!!' The parrot, Polly, an African Grey with a red tail and excellent speaking voice, was a present from one of her nurse's brothers who served in the Navy, and the bird brought a touch of exotica to the nursery. Every day he was let out of his cage to walk around the carpet until he 'dropped a card'. Dorothy found the

The young Dorothy with her toys.

Feb 1899

My darling Mother.
How do you like being
in Oxford? Have you
visited Old Tom yet?
I went to Earith this
afternoon, and Mrs Hard
gave me an orange, I ran
all the way with my
hoop. I am going to have a
violin practice with Daddy
when I have done my letter.
I am almost sorry I have got
a holiday from dictation.
Jacko is quite well and so
is Jocko, he is good but Jacko

is still naughty.
Give my best love to
Margaret and ask her
when she is coming to
Bluntisham again, tell her
I want her to come.
I am sending you a few
snowdrops with my best
love.
Now good bye darling
Mother from
your loving little
Dorothy

A letter from Dorothy to her mother in Oxford, 1899.

ritual loathsome: it was the 'exaggerated excitement of the grown-ups which impressed the incident so forcibly on my memory'.

Performance of all kinds was an integral part of rectory life and every member of the household had their allotted part. The Revd Sayers had his parochial duties, his wife a reluctant supporting role, but inside the rectory Dorothy stepped up to provide the entertainment for her parents, grandmother, aunts and any other visitors. 'I dramatized myself,' she later recalled, 'and have at all periods of my life continued to dramatize myself, into a great number of egotistical impersonations of a very common type, making myself the heroine (or, more often, the hero) of countless dramatic situations; but at all times, with a perfect realization that I was the creator and not the subject of these fantasies.' This was in stark contrast to the more disturbed inventions of the troubled Tennyson offspring who, unlike the self-empowered Dorothy, were not equipped to make this distinction, much to their detriment.

In her very young years, Dorothy recalled being asked to perform her 'toe-sucking' party piece, or to totter through the great arch of her father's legs, when visitors appeared in the drawing room. Another role was played out in the nightly ritual of going up to bed, cited in 'Cat O'Mary':

> Good-night, Mamma, good-night Papa,
> Good-night to all the rest;
> Good-night, Mamma, good-night, Papa,
> I must love Dolly best.

The adults waited in the hall with a mixture of pride, amusement and a 'certain nervousness', detectable to the precocious Katherine Lammas (the fictional Dorothy), to see whose name was to replace 'Dolly' as the favoured member of the household that day, the rhyme becoming a barometer of her fluctuating affections.

Being such a focus of adult attention and adulation necessarily had a profound and not always positive effect on the young Dorothy. Throughout her life she had a highly developed sense of her own importance that was grounded in her superior intellect and education. Looking back, the adult Dorothy almost despises her younger self, giving 'Cat O'Mary' the subtitle 'The Biography of a Prig', and she surmises that she must have been irritating to anyone outside her indulgent family circle.

With her mother often away in Oxford, much of the young Dorothy's time was spent under the direction of her father. There were moments of frivolity – the building of a snowman in the garden, for example, the dog cavorting around them – but for the most part her education was a serious affair. Henry Sayers was a dutiful and not a humorous man. The church organist maintained that she never saw him smile, and, unlike the fussy, kindly Mr Venables, the rector in *The Nine Tailors*, he kept a certain distance from his parishioners, insisting that the villagers touch their hat to him when they met him on the road. Helen found her virtuous, musical, book-loving rector husband dull. 'He bored her to death for nearly forty years,' Dorothy would comment unsparingly after her father's death. 'And she always grumbled that he was no companion for her,' before adding wryly and not without exasperation, 'and now she misses him dreadfully.'

Dorothy began learning the violin when she was 4, taught by her father who had made up his mind that his daughter would be musical, like all the Sayers. Ever willing to please, she applied herself diligently to her instrument and was rewarded with the satisfaction of performing at a local concert, where her superior playing was acknowledged with a call for two encores. The violin lessons took place in the rector's book-lined study, entrance to which was always preceded by knocking; this was the one male sanctum in a house filled with female relations. Here the Revd Sayers would accompany his daughter's violin on his American organ, and then, alone, compose his sermons and hymns and listen out for the bells of Bluntisham, wistfully recalling the sound of Great Tom's nightly ringing back at Christ Church, the only aspect of Oxford life he genuinely seems to have missed: 'often, in the seclusion of my country rectory, I recall them with regret,' he mused in his memoir.

At an early age Dorothy showed a gift for languages and from when she was 6 Latin instruction also took place in the study. She rapidly perfected the future simple of 'malo' and was rewarded with a penny, and learned the intricacies of old-style pronunciation, still prevalent in Oxford, as demonstrated by the pun: 'Why are the sailors [*nautae*] wicked? Because they are *nautae* [naughty]!' By 10 she was practically fluent in French and proficient in German, taught by a governess. Occasionally, as a special treat and break from lessons, her father allowed her to open the mysterious and lovely box on his desk and reverently take out his masonic regalia to try on. This was a solemn ritual, but then dressing up was never a frivolous pastime for Dorothy, she *was* the character she played: in 'Cat O' Mary', if an adult asked 'Are you going to dress up?' Katherine Lammas responded 'I'm going to *dress*' and observed that 'It was impossible to make these people understand that the character ... was more real to her than her own.' For Dorothy, literary fact and fiction were quite distinguishable but for dramatic purposes she inhabited the fictional persona completely.

The morning room was on the other side of the dining room. This was a narrow, surprisingly gloomy room decorated with a light green patterned paper and with a black wainscot. Here, in the company of her older female relatives, Dorothy absorbed a different kind of wisdom, but not one that would facilitate her entry into the wider society of adolescent girls later on. Dorothy's aunt and grandmother and any visiting 'entertaining' aunts would retire to this room after breakfast and again after dinner for knitting, crocheting and discussion. These endless conversations focused on Dorothy, or matters of health, or the inevitable parish concerns, all accompanied by the click of needles and overseen by the legend carved across the chimney-piece: 'Cheerful Hearts Make Cheerful Hearths.' Here Dorothy, aged just 6, managed to read aloud to Grannie and Mab (Aunt Mabel) the whole of a leading article on the relief of Ladysmith in the Boer War, and was proud enough of this achievement to mention it in a letter to her mother in Oxford. Such events in the outside world were of passing interest, however, and did not impinge on life at Bluntisham Rectory, where the focus was turned inwards to the domestic and the parochial.

The intense atmosphere inevitably produced disagreements of a very feminine kind. These were later depicted with salty wit in 'Cat O' Mary', where one aunt's imagined internal growth is dismissed by the doctor as a mere inflammation of the bowel. She is put out by his lack of concern and use of such explicit language: '"Horrid ill-mannered little man," said Miss Warwick. "I don't want to be told about my – bowel. It's not nice."' 'Why shouldn't you have bowels like everybody else?' replies the straight-talking Great-aunt Agatha. 'Good old English world, bowel.' Such a forthright exchange was possible only in a confined environment where familial and domestic discord formed part of the necessary shading for those with no outside stimulation. Disagreement could be introduced because all the participants knew it would be resolved.

Long evenings were spent in this constricted room, illuminated only by candles and dreary paraffin lamps emitting more suffocating smells than light.

Left to right: Dorothy's cousin Ivy Shrimpton, the Revd and Mrs Sayers, and Dorothy.

The focus was inevitably narrow and the atmosphere stifling, a startling contrast to the howling winds that blew across the Fens. As Dorothy cast her dramatic eye beyond the nursery, the entertaining female relatives were only too willing to emerge from the morning room to take up their allotted parts in her theatrical productions; despite the exacting direction by Dorothy, such moments were a welcome distraction.

Dorothy did not mix well with children of her own age. In later life she admitted, 'I never cared at all for children, nor have I, at any time of my life, liked the company of people younger than myself. Perhaps this comes of being an only child.' She did not form close friendships with even the occasional young visitor to the rectory. One of these was Guy Cooke, the younger brother of a former pupil of the Revd Sayers at the Choir School, who boarded at the rectory for a year and shared lessons with Dorothy (providing an extra income for the rector). In scholarly terms Dorothy found him substandard, measuring her own accomplishments against his only confirmed her own superiority. Although they shared nursery games reasonably happily, fashioning armour and adorning shields with noble mottoes – 'To Glory or to Death' – it was not a friendship. When Cooke died in the First World War he was not greatly mourned by Dorothy who, although she could act most parts with aplomb, could not bring herself to fake an emotion she did not feel. She suffered the same qualms when her grandmother died. Unable to feel genuine grief she was relieved when her mother did not insist she accompany her to the funeral conducted by her father at Bluntisham church just across the lane.

The arrival at the rectory of Dorothy's cousin Ivy changed everything. Ivy Shrimpton, the daughter of her mother's sister Amy, had been born in California but returned to England when the family's farm failed. She was eight years older than Dorothy, but for the first time in her life Dorothy felt she had an ally. Ivy introduced her to Louisa M. Alcott's *Little Women*, Richard Harris Barham's *Ingoldsby Legends*, and possessed a view of the world that allowed her to accept the admonishments of her younger, rather priggish cousin with equanimity. 'I think, old girl, that you are just a bit inclined to form a harsh judgement – or perhaps I ought rather to say, a hard judgement of other people,' Dorothy once told her. 'I shouldn't like to feel, Ivy, that supposing some time I sinned a great sin, that I should be afraid to come to you for help.' Ironically, it was to Ivy that Dorothy learned to reveal any secret selves, however unpalatable, well into adulthood.

They bicycled, shared confidences and giggled about a young visitor to the rectory, Arthur Hutchinson, nicknamed Dull Red (after his choice of croquet ball), and discussed the serious matters of Creationism and Phariseeism. During the magical summer of 1907 the girls discovered Dumas's *The Three Musketeers* and Bluntisham was transformed into the Château de Bragelonne. Dorothy was Athos, the handsome nobleman with a tragic past, the Revd Sayers was King Louis, her mother Cardinal Richelieu, the governess D'Artagnan, and the French au pair took the part of Porthos, with Ivy cast as Marie, Duchesse de Chevreuse, friend, lover and confidante of Athos. It was an intense and long-running production. Costumes were carefully constructed – 'We have been hard at work making a curly wig for Porthos,' she told Ivy, 'as of course his hair is too long' – and Dorothy's bedroom became known as her 'quarters', the walls covered with her drawings of swords, hats and musketeers on horseback. His Eminence (Helen Sayers) had provided a rug and cushion that made the room very well appointed, and hung over her writing table were her little ornaments of devils. 'I use them, for the nonce,' she wrote to Ivy, 'as a rest for my quill-pens, to show to whom I have dedicated my writings!!'

Such an existence could not be sustained. Dorothy was outgrowing the rarefied atmosphere of Bluntisham and was to be sent to school. 'I am leaving the Court,' she wrote to Ivy in June 1908, 'and going far away. I am going to School! Out and alas! for our noble company. The grand bond will be broken for ever after Christmas! for ever and ever. And now, no more shall the Four Musketeers walk side by side in the garden, or fight together for the King.'

It was not quite the end for the Musketeers, however, as for several years she continued to address her parents in letters home as members of the court, signing herself 'Athos'. Godolphin School in Salisbury was a successful choice from an academic point of view but socially Dorothy struggled. Her singular nature and isolated upbringing had not equipped her with the skills to fit in with the peculiarly hothouse atmosphere of a girls' boarding school. One of her few friends was Molly Edmondson, another daughter of the rectory from 'somewhere in the Black Country', who shared Dorothy's love of the stage and poetry. According to Dorothy, Molly was considered a 'weird freak, like me' by the conventional portion of the Godolphin establishment. After a serious bout of measles Dorothy's hair fell out and this, coupled with a long absence to recuperate, signified the beginning of the end of her school career. In December 1911 it was decided she would prepare for her Oxford entrance examinations

Dorothy in her teens dressed as Athos. She was entranced by *The Three Musketeers*, which she began reading in French at the age of 13.

from home rather than return to Godolphin, and in March 1912 she sat successfully for a scholarship to Somerville College.

Dorothy threw herself into life at Oxford, reporting her myriad academic, theatrical and musical activities in long, detailed letters back to the rectory. Surprisingly, at the end of her second year, in the summer of 1914, with war looming, Dorothy and her friend Elsie Henderson, chaperoned by a Miss Lawrence, embarked on a trip to France, where they intended to spend six weeks. Dorothy wrote home from Tours on 2 August, rather taken aback at the level of mobilization all around them: 'Yesterday we went into the town here ... It was most extraordinary. Everybody one met seemed to be in a fearful hurry ... Soldiers and sailors were all over the place ... I do hope we shall be able to stay, because it is so fearfully thrilling.' But after witnessing locals being rounded up as suspected spies and learning that a curé had been shot as a traitor (he had allegedly concealed plans of the area in his bicycle tyre), the gravity of the situation finally penetrated. War was declared on 4 August but it was not until 25 August that the party returned home.

The reality of war finally reached Bluntisham Rectory in the summer of 1915 in the form of an uncle and a cousin who came for a visit. Traumatized by their experiences at the front, both of them had had nervous breakdowns, and were, not surprisingly, 'uncommonly gloomy'. 'I'm rather glad they're gone,' Dorothy wrote to her friend Muriel Jaeger, 'because I do so hate everlasting war-talk, and I'm always in terror of Mother getting another of her nervous attacks.' These attacks had in fact become severe. Unusually, Dorothy articulated her fears for her mother to Muriel: 'she loses control over her speech and limbs. Nothing very dreadful happened this time though, but it is always a most worrying possibility.' Dorothy's maternal relations were 'everlastingly tied up inside or dosing themelves', and Helen's nervous disposition increasingly presented itself with alarming, epileptic symptoms, episodes that Dorothy did her best to prevent.

War changed everything: 'since then we been all topsy-turvy, like' remarks the sexton Harry Gotobed in *The Nine Tailors*. The certainties of the old order were swept away, and even inside the rectories of the most secluded of parishes things would never be the same again. This 'topsy-turvy' world was one in which educated women such as Dorothy and her character Miss Thorpe in *The Nine Tailors* might carve an independent path. It was not, however, one in which the Revd Sayers would play an active part. In 1917 he exchanged the comparatively wealthy parish of Bluntisham for the living of Christchurch, a name with nostalgic appeal, but even more removed from the gleaming spires of Oxford. It entailed a further withdrawal into the Fens and the Sayers lived there until the rector's death in 1928, with occasional visits from Dorothy, who found its position of profound isolation depressing: 'the last place God made, and when He'd finished he found He'd forgotten the staircase!' she complained in a letter to Eric Whelpton, an Oxford friend.

Nonetheless, for Dorothy, the safe, ordered rectory of her childhood was the backdrop to her exploration of the mysterious and murderous in a series of detective novels in the late 1920s and early 1930s. In her hands, the innocent secrets of everyday life were turned on their head and became something much more sinister in the conventional context of an Oxford women's college (*Gaudy Night*), a gentlemen's club (*The Unpleasantness at the Bellona Club*) or a Fenland parish (*The Nine Tailors*). As the controlling narrator she ensured order was restored, a process informed by her familiarity with Christian doctrine. The setting of the 'Great Good Place' for murderous crimes was used by other writers, such as Agatha Christie, during the golden age of detective fiction in the 1920s and 1930s. As W. H. Auden pointed out, 'the more Eden-like it is, the greater the contradiction of murder'. The corpse must shock not only because it is a dead body but also because it is 'shockingly out of place, as when a dog makes a mess on a drawing-room carpet'.

While Dorothy – a woman 'brimful of the energy of a well-stocked mind', according to Doreen Wallace, an Oxford contemporary – was creating the characters of Lord Peter Wimsey and Harriet Vane, she was playing out her own domestic drama, unhappily but stoically. The intimacy established with her cousin Ivy in the Bluntisham Rectory enabled Dorothy to keep the greatest secret of her life: the existence of an illegitimate son, John Anthony, born in 1924, whom Ivy brought up and whose true identity was revealed only after Dorothy's death. Her hope that she might 'adopt' him and bring him up herself once she married the journalist 'Mac' Fleming in 1926, was thwarted by her husband's mental instability, stemming from service in the First World War. It was not a happy marriage, although the couple stayed together until Mac's death in 1950.

Dorothy gave up writing detective fiction in the mid-1930s and today her literary reputation also rests on her theological writings and her work as a critic and translator. She was working on the third and final volume of a verse translation of Dante's *Divine Comedy* at the time of her death in December 1957.

CHAPTER FOUR

Guardians of that Holy Land

Rupert Brooke at Grantchester

I N 1909, AS THE SAYERS FAMILY was living out the last hurrah of the Edwardian rectory in splendid isolation on the edge of the Fens, thirteen miles away in Cambridge, Rupert Brooke (1887–1915), an aspiring poet and temporarily thwarted academic, was searching for lodgings in the area.

Social distractions had interfered with his studies and he now sought a calmer environment in which to write his dissertation on John Webster. The ambitious, charismatic son of a Rugby schoolmaster, Brooke had already established a name for himself at the university as an actor, poet and leading light in the Fabian Society, but his failure to obtain a First in Finals had been a disappointment both to him and to his formidable mother. Determined to salvage his academic career and consolidate his chances of a fellowship at King's College, he contemplated taking rooms at Grantchester, two miles upstream from Cambridge itself.

Grantchester, mentioned in the Domesday Book, was a small, quiet community. Most of the villagers worked on the land or in the flour mill over the river, transport was still primarily by horse and cart, water was drawn up from wells and light provided by candles or oil lamps. But the place was well known to Cambridge undergraduates as a destination for walks, punting outings and picnics, with tea in the garden at the Orchard provided by Mrs Stevenson, who had lived at Orchard House since 1891. She was popular with the students and by the time Brooke joined their ranks she was offering dawn breakfast on the banks of the Cam, or Granta as it is known at this point, to the all-night revellers

Punting on the Cam near Grantchester in the early twentieth century.

of May Day. Indeed, it was at Orchard House, previously part of the neighbour-ing Old Vicarage's working farm buildings, that Brooke first took lodgings, before taking up residence in the Old Vicarage itself in the early spring of 1911, staying there until 1912.

For Brooke, the attractions of Grantchester were readily identified: it was at a relatively safe distance from his urban haunts, yet close enough for access to libraries and tutors. More importantly for the young poet, it was the ideal venue in which to play host to an eclectic group of friends. Grantchester life suited him. Although his tenure at this most romantic of Cambridgeshire parishes was brief, it was here, and in the Old Vicarage in particular, that he was to find his spiritual home and the perfect backdrop to his writing.

'This is a deserted, lonely, dank, ruined, overgrown, gloomy, lovely house,' he would write to his cousin Erica Cotterill of the Old Vicarage, 'and fusty with the ghosts of generations of mouldering clergymen. It is a fit place to write my kind of poetry in.' His excitement at finding his own *genius loci* – a place with a particular resonance for him and his writing – is palpable. Here was a ready-made, peculiarly English scene composed of a sense of gothic drama, a tint of age (the vicarage already 'the old vicarage') and indeed eternity – 'the ghosts of generations' – against which the golden boy Rupert and his poetry would be thrown into sharp relief.

Although the grandson, on his mother's side, of a vicar, Brooke was a self-declared 'agnogger', in the Cambridge terminology of the time, detached from what he described in a letter to his friend Jacques Raverat as 'the pale serene Anglican windless harmonium-buzzing Eternity of the Christians'. However, the Old Vicarage, as eulogized in his eponymous poem of 1912, was central to his vision of England. It was a place in which a poet's and indeed a nation's nostalgic yearning for a spiritual and emotional home ('Home' was the poem's original title) was anchored, a safe haven from the tide of modernization and, in due course, the horrors of industrial warfare.

Brooke was not the first to identify and defend the pastoral seclusion of Grantchester. When he took up lodgings there in 1909, several dons were already living in the parish and zealously guarding their piece of England from encroaching urbanization, even signing a petition to register their concerns about a proposed new housing development in the village. This impulse to stop time was, of course, a rearguard action – 'Stands the Church clock at ten to three?' is the famous line from 'The Old Vicarage, Grantchester' – an attempt to preserve a dream at a time when the world order was bent on its destruction.

In 1380 Corpus Christi, a newly founded Cambridge college, acquired the advowson of the living of Grantchester. This meant it received the income from the rectorial lands and had the power to appoint the residing vicar. The first master of the college, Thomas de Eltisley, gave the incumbent a vicarage with two acres and a rood and a half of land. The usual history of struggles with dilapidations plus the occasional dissolute vicar too keen on the ale house followed, until, after the decay wrought by the Civil War, a new vicarage, the essence of the Old Vicarage today, was built by the Revd Shortynge around 1683 (the date was originally carved into one of the doorposts in an upper room of the Old Vicarage but is no longer visible). The Archdeacon's visitations of 1685 describe a 'good, new-built vicaridge house' alongside a 'good handsome church … in good order'. It also records, with some relief, 'the minister resides'.

This house was still in existence at the end of the Revd William Butts's incumbency in the early nineteenth century. By 1828, it was being advertised to let, the vicar preferring to live in the parish of Little Wilbraham nearby. By 1850, after being neglected by successive tenants, the vicarage was deemed unfit for the incoming Revd William Martin, a Fellow of Corpus Christi College. This exacting gentleman cleric sniffily declared the building 'cold and damp', demanding instead all the necessary trappings for a man of his social standing and distinction, including additional stables.

Thus abandoned (the Revd Martin built himself a fine new rectory on land purchased with help from Queen Anne's Bounty and a generous grant from Corpus), the vicarage now became the Old Vicarage. In 1851 it fell into the eager hands of Samuel Page Widnall (known as Page), a keen photographer, amateur historian, model maker and dahlia grower, who acquired the freehold of the now 'tumbledown vicarage', as the Revd Joseph Romilly, Registrary of the University of Cambridge, described it, with its forlorn garden and glebe. After a programme of refurbishment, Page moved in with his wife, Lily, in 1853. They were joined by his sister Lally in 1854, and this triumvirate (there were no children) lived happily at the Old Vicarage as watchful and sympathetic custodians for the next forty years.

Page Widnall was a man of many parts; he wrote his own history of Grantchester, printing it on his homemade Widnall press, housed off the kitchen. He also left an idiosyncratic architectural legacy in the shape of the Castle Ruin, a Gothic folly built in 1857 near the mill stream at the end of the garden. The folly was only one of his architectural creations. The Swiss cottage, bathing house and dovecote may have been lost over time, but Widnall's sundial and fountain still remain as testaments to his romantic, not to say eccentric, disposition. It was 'a place straight out of a fairy tale', according to one contemporary, and Lally declared it to be 'the sweetest garden the sun ever shone upon in all our dear Merry England'.

Widnall's workshop was in his Gothic folly. He worked in wood and stone, or with whatever was to hand (his candelabra, which now stands in the nave of Grantchester church, was made out of cake tins). His skill as a draughtsman found expression in his models of buildings and intricately constructed doll's houses of card and plaster, complete with detailed furnishings of the Old Vicarage of his day. From a tiny, delicate model, we see the house as it was in the 1870s, largely unchanged from the 'vicaridge house' of 1683. It is symmetrical in shape, one room deep with two massive chimneystacks at either end, weighty anchors for this long narrow building (the largest stack originally measured 9 × 7 feet at ground-floor level). The main door of the house was at the centre of the western elevation, leading straight out of the drawing room into the magical garden. This room was the location for Widnall's sister Lally's schoolroom, where she educated the local children, including Polly (Mary) Greene, a landscape artist who counted among her pupils Gwen Darwin (later Raverat), Brooke's intimate friend and a frequent visitor to the Old Vicarage during his brief tenure. Raverat's fine 1937 wood engraving of the chestnut trees ranged along the Granta outside the house captures and frames this piece of Brooke's poetic vision.

Widnall's photographs allow us a glimpse into domestic life at the Old Vicarage during these late Victorian years, with family gatherings on the lawn and theatricals in the Castle Ruin all adding texture to a contented existence. 'We were very happy, my dear, and the best of it was – we knew we were happy,' Lally was to remark later to a friend. With her death in 1908 (Lily had died in 1886 and Page in 1894) the merry existence of the Widnall era ended. The house then passed to Lally's niece Mrs Emily Giles who never lived in it but let it, furnished, to Henry and Florence Neeve and their son, Cyril. Henry Neeve was a carpenter at the firm of Arthur Negus of Cambridge. He and his wife were not perhaps as well-to-do as the Widnalls, but their aesthetic sensibility is hinted at in Florence Neeve's noted fondness for old houses and in descriptions

The Widnall family: Lily, Lally and Page on the back lawn of the Old Vicarage, Grantchester, *c.* 1863.

Above: The front of the Old Vicarage, *c.* 1910.
Below: The earliest surviving photograph of the Old Vicarage, *c.* 1860,
showing the view of the house from the garden.

made by their observant neighbour, Rupert Brooke, when he was lodging next door at the Orchard.

When Lytton Strachey was considering taking rooms at the Old Vicarage in 1909, Brooke was already on hand to describe Strachey's potential landlords. Although they were 'working-people', the Rugby-educated classicist observed, Mr Neeve had an 'accent above his class' and an appetite for botany, 'advanced newspapers' and honey from his own beehives. Brooke had spied this surprisingly (to him) refined character sitting in his garden reading these advanced newspapers near the beehives with a handkerchief over his head. Brooke reported back to Strachey, his fellow Apostle, that the Neeves were seeking lodgers to help pay for the education of their only son.

Brooke was already constructing his own lyrical imaginings around the Old Vicarage from his vantage point at the Orchard. For him, the triumph of the Old Vicarage was the garden. He was happy to inform Strachey that 'I greatly recommend all the outside of The Old Vicarage. In the autumn it will be very Ussher-like [sic]. There are trees rather too closely all round; and a mist. It's right on the river, I nearly went there: but I could find no reason for deserting my present place. It's only the inside of the house I don't know about. I put Jacques [Raverat] there for a week … and he seemed happy. But he's very wild. The cooking mightn't be *good*. But I think they're cleanish and docile.' As with the house in Edgar Allan Poe's tale 'The Fall of the House of Usher' (1839), Brooke sensed a quasi-human presence of spectral diners in the gothic atmosphere of the old crumbling building and its overgrown garden.

Despite not having lived at the Orchard at that point for very long – he moved there in the early summer of 1909 – Brooke was already adopting a proprietorial air. Life at Grantchester was suiting the young poet well. Familiar with the village from outings while an undergraduate, he had occasionally entertained friends to tea at Mrs Stevenson's popular tea garden. Her husband was a working dairyman and part of the building was still an apple store with a stable below when Brooke took lodgings there. The rooms at the Orchard were small and functional, so Brooke spent much of that summer outside, barefoot, embracing his newly discovered sense of the pastoral life. 'I am in The Country, in Arcadia, a rustic,' he declared to Noel Olivier, the youthful – she was only 16 – youngest daughter of the leading civil servant and Fabian Sydney Olivier, and one of the young women with whom Brooke became emotionally involved in this period.

Although near to Cambridge, this place was a world away from the city and its 'dull bald spectacled people' who would occasionally invade the magical kingdom to take tea and be teased by Brooke who cast himself in a Puck-like role: 'I mock them & pour the cream down their necks or roll them in the rose-beds or push them in the river, & they hate me & go away,' he wrote to his cousin Erica.

The romantic construct takes on a life of its own in Brooke's correspondence. He conjures an idyllic loneliness, describing to Erica how he is in

> a sort of cottage, with a dear plump weather-beaten kindly old lady in control. I have a perfectly glorious time, seeing nobody I know day after day. The room I have opens straight out onto a stone verandah covered with creepers, & a little old garden full of old-fashioned flowers & *crammed* with roses. I work at Shakespere [*sic*], read, write all day, & now & then wander in the woods or by the river. I bathe every morning & sometimes by moonlight; have all my meals (chiefly fruit) brought to me out of doors, & am as happy as the day's long. I am chiefly sorry for all you people in the world.'

Conditions inside Orchard House were cramped. There was, Brooke conceded, no room to 'May' (celebrate May Day) inside his lodgings, 'but you might all sit on the floor and have tea,' he wrote to Gwen Darwin in May 1909. However, lack of space was no hindrance to Brooke, playing enthusiastic host to his extensive and eccentric acquaintance, as they were often outside, in the meadows or loaded up in his friend Justin Brooke's Opel motor car speeding along the Grantchester lanes. Most of the photographs from this time show Brooke and his companions punting, writing, camping, swimming, or wrestling, Lawrentian-like, in Grantchester meadows. This Eden-like existence extended to a nearby field where the artist Augustus John had established camp, living a more robust version of Brooke's pagan lifestyle in a caravan.

As the summer ended, an autumnal and languid sense of decay crept into his garden: 'the orchard is golden & melancholy and sleepy and enchanted. I sit neck deep in dead red leaves,' Brooke wrote to his friend and mentor Edward Marsh at the end of September 1909. Disease and death were in fact not far away. That winter Brooke became ill with suspected typhoid on his return from a trip to Klosters, and in January 1910, Brooke's father, in his penultimate term

Brooke's friends breakfasting in the garden of the Orchard, 1910. Seated from left to right: A.Y. Campbell, Jacques Raverat, Geoffrey Keynes, Hugh Morgan, Ethel Pye and Dudley Ward.

Cambridge picnic party near Byron's pool, 1908. Left to right: Frances Darwin,
Francis Cornford, Eva Spielman, Margery Olivier and Rupert Brooke.

as a housemaster at Rugby and just as he was about to retire in pensionable comfort, suffered a stroke and died on the very day the pupils were due to return for the spring term. Brooke's sense of filial duty took over and, reluctantly, he did not return to Grantchester but remained at Rugby to help his mother run the house.

This was a dismal time. Exiled from his own arcadia, he fell into a deep depression. Isolation at Rugby – 'I hate my family,' he wrote to his schoolfriend Geoffrey Keynes, and to the musicologist E. J. Dent he confessed, 'I've always felt so especially unlike and separate from my parents' – compared unfavourably with the happy solitude of the life he had made for himself at Grantchester. He was desperate. 'I love being there so much – much more than any place I've ever lived in,' he wrote in his misery to his friend Frances Cornford. 'Will you have a meal in the Meadows in May with me – i.e. honey under the Orchard apple-blossom?' he implored Gwen Darwin. In Rugby, up in the attic, 'the only room in the house a human being with an aesthetic soul can live in for an hour', he struggled to keep alive the sustaining vision of Grantchester, writing to Dudley Ward: 'I think … all of you are dreams I've had. It's so faint.'

By the spring of 1910 he had extricated himself from his filial duties in Rugby and returned to his lodgings at the Orchard and his 'pink Paradise of blossom', as he described it to Edward Marsh. With his 'dew-dabbling' friends he resumed a way of life that Virginia Stephen (later Woolf) famously described as 'Neo-Pagan'. The idyll continued through the summer of 1910, and he got up parties consisting of Justin and Jacques (Raverat), Ka Cox (a fellow member of the Fabian Society with whom he became romantically entangled), Margaret Darwin, Gwen Darwin and the Olivier sisters. Night-time sorties took place along the river to Cambridge with Brooke expertly guiding the punt back to Grantchester along the rivered darkness, deciphering landmarks by the rustle of the leaves on a particular overhanging tree.

A prominent member of the Cambridge Dramatic Society, Brooke positioned himself very carefully as the romantic hero on his own stage at Grantchester. Colonizing both the Orchard and the Old Vicarage next door, where the Pye girls (friends of the Oliviers) and Noel Olivier had taken rooms, the group held rehearsals for *Doctor Faustus* in the garden. With a performer's eye for staging (Henry James remarked on Brooke's 'scenic perfection'), Brooke would read *Paradise Lost* to his friends from the high branches of a chestnut tree. When the economist John Maynard Keynes arrived at the Old Vicarage one

Rupert Brooke as the Attendant Spirit in a student production of Milton's *Comus*, 1908.

Rupert Brooke, photographed in 1913 by Sherril Schell: 'Magnificently unprepared/For the long littleness of life' Frances Cornford wrote of him in 'Youth' (1910).

evening he was met by the sight of Brooke 'sitting in the midst of admiring females with nothing on but an embroidered sweater'.

When the group gathered in the small, low-ceilinged sitting room at the Old Vicarage it felt as if they had been cast adrift in a ship's cabin. To the infatuated Sybil Pye, Brooke, silhouetted in the soft glow cast by the lamp as he sat with his book, was an object of wonder. She marvelled at his 'outline and proportions of forehead, cheek and chin' with their 'complete and unusual dignity'. These are the recognizable features of the young yet immortal Greek god he had come to represent in his charmed circle. Such evenings often ended with a late-night swim, the water 'sweet and cool', as described in 'The Old Vicarage'. Afterwards, strolling up to the house from the river through the row of chestnuts – 'A tunnel of green gloom' – Brooke would hang upside down from a poplar tree to dry his long hair, a pose that reminded the watchful Sybil of a William Blake woodcut.

There was a self-consciousness about the magical quality of Grantchester and all it represented even as they were living out the arcadian idyll. Gwen Darwin lamented its passing even while she was part of the immediate experience, writing to Frances Cornford in August 1910: 'I wish one of us would write a "Ballade des beaux jours à Grantchester". I can't bear to think of all these young beautiful people getting old and tired and stiff in the joints … If one of those afternoons could be written down, just as it was exactly, it would be a poem – but I suppose perhaps a thoroughly *lived* poem can't be written.'

Edward Thomas and E. M. Forster were among Brooke's autumn visitors. He continued with his poetry and dined in Cambridge with, among others, the poet and Fellow of Magdalene College A. C. Benson, but the Stevensons were tiring of Booke's unusual lifestyle. Frustration was mutual: there were 'horrible people' in his house, Brooke complained to his mother, and by December he had arranged to transfer to the Old Vicarage, where he had in any case spent so much of the summer. The rooms allotted to him by Mrs Neeve were at the centre of the house, the doors leading out into the garden, with his bedroom above, from where he could see past Widnall's fountain, down to the river. For these three rooms, two on the ground floor and one above, plus full board, he paid thirty shillings a week.

After spending time in Europe in early 1911, Brooke returned to Grantchester to take up residence at the Old Vicarage. Friends continued to be drawn to his Eden. Edward Marsh visited in July, writing afterwards that 'the food is simple and extremely unwholesome' and describing how they passed the time: 'One talks eight hours, reads eight, and sleeps eight.' Brooke's writing was going well and, through Marsh, he found a publisher, Frank Sidgwick, for his first book of poems. The contract was signed on 12 August 1911 and witnessed by Virginia Stephen during her week-long stay in Grantchester. Days were spent absorbed in writing, Brooke on his dissertation and his poems, Virginia on what would become *The Voyage Out* (1915). One evening Brooke invited Virginia to join him for some nude bathing in Byron's pool, a spot he favoured with its association to that earlier Romantic Cambridge poet. She found the experience thrilling but was subsequently rather disappointed that her fellow members of the Bloomsbury group were not more shocked by such a daring disregard for propriety.

The river remained a constant presence, later transposed in his imagination into something with restorative and morally cleansing properties, as he observed to Geoffrey Keynes in June of the following year: 'I haven't bathed since November. There's a lot to wash off.' The young David Garnett, a friend of the Oliviers, who visited Brooke in the summers of 1910 and 1911, recalled the river's elemental aspects in his memoir, *The Golden Echo* (1953): 'We went about midnight ... out of the garden of the Old Vicarage into the lane full of thick white dust ... we walked noiselessly in our sand-shoes, and then through the dew-soaked grass of the meadow ... to bathe naked in the unseen water, smelling of wild peppermint and mud.'

In December 1911 *Poems* was published, albeit with some enforced changes. There had been change, too, in paradise. The harsher reality of living the rural dream was becoming apparent to Brooke. That summer he had begun to notice that although the house was one of the loveliest, it was also one of the 'unhealthiest ... one could imagine', infested with woodlice. He had taken to sleeping outside on the lawn but would be woken at 2.30 a.m. by birds singing, his hair damp and cold from the dew. Brooke's interior life seemed to be echoed in the gloomy spaces of the Old Vicarage, where heavy rain kept him trapped, as he wrote to Noel Olivier, 'in an infinitely dark room'.

The Old Vicarage was losing some of its magnetism. The charmed circle of Grantchester was disintegrating. Ka Cox declared her love for the artist Henry Lamb and spurned Brooke. Devastated, the poet, who was already suffering from mental exhaustion, blamed Lytton Strachey for orchestrating the relationship and scheming against him. It was a schism that would never be

Dudley Ward and Rupert Brooke on the Cam, *c.* 1910.

healed. Breaking with Bloomsbury, and in the midst of nervous collapse, Brooke fled to the Continent in early 1912 to recover his equanimity.

He headed for Berlin where his university friend Dudley Ward was living. There, the image of the halcyon days of youth and innocence at Grantchester rose up before him. It was in this mood of contemplative longing and in search of the certainties of 'Home' that Brooke wrote 'The Old Vicarage, Grantchester'. He had been reading Hilaire Belloc's rhapsody on rural Sussex, 'Duncton Hill':

> He does not die that can bequeath
> Some influence to the land he knows,
> Or dares, persistent, interwreath
> Love permanent with the wild hedgerows.

The sentiment resonated with Brooke, summoning everything he held so dear as he sat scribbling in the Café des Westens in urban Berlin: 'That river and the chestnuts – came back to me a lot. Tea on the lawn,' as he wrote to Ka Cox. He had been away from Grantchester for several months, but the outline of his pastoral dream emerged on the page with perfect clarity.

He despatched the poem (a 'masterpiece', he confidently declared) to England, just in time to make the June 1912 issue of *Basileon*, the King's College magazine. The 'long lanky lax-limbed set of verses', as he later described it to Sybil Pye, was positively received, and confirmed Brooke's position as one of the leading Georgian poets. From a distance he had begun to doubt the Old Vicarage's very existence, writing to Geoffrey Keynes: 'The mind of man decays & grows uncertain with disease & the quiet lapse of time, & I had become more than a little doubtful if it had ever happened that I was in such a place, or if I had but dreamt it.' Returning to Grantchester in late June he was relieved to find it all unchanged. On the first afternoon he was back, Mrs Neeve brought his tea tray out into the garden with the announcement that there was 'still honey for tea, Mr Brooke!' She was quoting from the end of the poem – 'Stands the Church clock at ten to three?/And is there honey still for tea?' – lines that would in due course make the village of Grantchester internationally famous. ('Ten to three' was a mere rhyming device, as the hands of the church clock were broken and stuck at 7.45 until the 1920s, when it was finally mended.)

However, the Neo-Pagan romance, lived with such fervour for the last few summers, was hard to rekindle. The overgrown garden was 'immeasurably autumnal, sad, mysterious, august', as he wrote to Marsh, and seemed to reflect his melancholy. The woodlice had returned with a vengeance. Brooke gazed up at them nightly as they emerged punctually at 10 p.m. from their two caverns by each window to explore the walls and ceiling, 'its glades and peaks … extraordinarily romantic to them'. Brooke's solitude now became loneliness, a kind of accidie exacerbated by a lack of sleep. The spectral vicars and dusty curates dancing on the lawn in 'The Old Vicarage' were, in his mind, exacting revenge on him: 'When I get to bed I'm a mere rag, and since I was told about the ghost – I've been able to do nothing but lie awake wet with terror,' he told his intimate friend from Rugby and fellow Apostle, James Strachey. By July 1912 he was declaring himself 'sick of Grantchester'. Perhaps he was sick of himself, and the salve of Grantchester was no longer able to heal him. He was, he moaned to Geoffrey Keynes, suffering from a 'syphilis of the soul'.

By autumn 1912 he had left Grantchester. Exhausted mentally and physically, further disillusioned and with his friendships and emotional life in turmoil, he departed England altogether in the spring of 1913 on a year-long odyssey that would encompass the new worlds of Canada, the United States, the South Seas and New Zealand. It was a trip partly financed by commissioned articles about his travels. In North America, he found himself unable to assimilate the vast scale of the landscape into poetry. The feeling of being anchorless was beginning to trouble him and 'misty, rather mad, slightly moral, shy & lovely' English pastoral thoughts began to crowd his mind. In early March 1914 he wrote to Edward Marsh from Tahiti of his longing to be 'tied to somewhere in England. I can't do this vagabondage'. Shortly afterwards, he began the return voyage and was turning over thoughts of home in a series of poems, including 'The Treasure', printed later that year:

Still may Time hold some golden space
    Where I'll unpack that scented store
Of song and flower and sky and face,
    And count, and touch, and turn them o'er,
Musing upon them […]

Brooke did not return to Grantchester. England was heading for war, which was declared on 4 August 1914. In mid-September, he obtained a commission in the Royal Naval Division through the influence of Edward Marsh, private secretary to Winston Churchill, now First Lord of the Admiralty. With the prospect of going into action, the need to preserve the 'golden space' of the Old Vicarage pressed in on his mind. On hearing reports while training that it was to be demolished, Brooke rattled off a note to Frances Cornford marked 'IMPORTANT': 'Awful rumours prevail here that the Old Vicarage is to be destroyed. I wonder if you could find out if that's so; by whose orders; & what steps could be taken in the way of saving it. I mean, could one buy it, or the land? It seems to me very important. Failing that, I want some decent painter to make a picture of it.' The prospect of his poetic space being destroyed brought back into focus the importance he attached to it as a place of innocence, poetic inspiration and, above all, hope. The rumour proved to be false. 'It shall yet be left for that slower Prussian, Time, to reduce it,' Brooke wrote to E. J. Dent with palpable relief. 'Perhaps I may buy it with my prize-money, after the war.'

By October Brooke had been deployed to Belgium. Marching through the shelled houses, the dead men and horses of Antwerp lit up by the glare from the lakes and rivers of burning petrol, he felt he was in a 'Dantesque Hell'. But later he saw 'a truer Hell. Hundreds of thousands of refugees, their goods on barrows and hand-carts and perambulators and waggons, moving with infinite slowness out into the night ... the old men mostly weeping, the women with hard white drawn faces.'

Six months later he was dead. He contracted blood poisoning as his division was on its way to Gallipoli and he died at sea on 23 April. The Apollo of English poetry was buried in an olive grove on the island of Skyros. He prefigured his loss in the famous opening lines of his poem 'The Soldier' (1914):

> If I should die, think only this of me:
>> That there's some corner of a foreign field
> That is forever England.

In 1916, his redoubtable mother, who had by now lost all three of her sons (one from pneumonia in 1907, the other, Alfred, in Flanders in June 1915), purchased the freehold of the Old Vicarage for £750. The following year it was put in trust so that Brooke's great friend Dudley Ward could make it his family home. It was Mrs Brooke's express wish that the house should remain as it was when her son lived there: the 'messuage where he had written so many of his Poems and other literary works, [to be] kept in their existing state so that the same may remain as a memorial of the said Rupert Chawner Brooke.' The Ward family honoured the house's literary tradition, cramming books into every conceivable space. Dudley's son Peter used the Gothic folly as a workshop, restoring musical boxes and automata and crafting delicate wooden toys and scientific instruments, so continuing Page Widnall's legacy of invention. The next incumbents, Lord and Lady Archer, who bought the house in 1979, are still 'doing their bit for Brooke', hosting the centenary celebration of the writing of 'The Old Vicarage, Grantchester' in May 2012.

Forty years after Brooke's death, the myth perpetuated by 'The Old Vicarage, Grantchester' seduced Ted Hughes and Sylvia Plath when they became lovers. Self-consciously these two poets laid their claim to Brooke's legacy, retracing his footsteps, a literary pilgrimage that particularly appealed to the young American Fulbright scholar at Cambridge. In April 1956, two months after she first met Hughes, Sylvia wrote home to her mother: 'All gathers in incredible joy. I cannot stop writing poems! They come from the vocabulary of woods and animals and earth that Ted is teaching me. We walked fifteen miles yesterday through woods, field, and fen, and came home through moonlit Gran[t]chester and fields of sleeping cows.' Two weeks later they were sharing tea and honey under the apple tree and the ever-watchful gaze of Brooke's church clock.

The couple's later attempts to live out the dream in an old farmhouse neighbouring the church in North Tawton, in deepest Devon, were shortlived. Plath's poetic vocabulary turned increasingly morbid as their marriage disintegrated; friendly villagers morph into the unrecognizable and threatening strangers of her poem 'The Bee Meeting' (1962), and the gentle undulating hills of the Devon countryside are transposed into the bleak interior landscape of her later poems. Hughes himself, through the darkness of Plath's breakdown and eventual suicide, continued to search for a way to translate the myth of England that had so inspired him at Grantchester.

Through his famous poem, Brooke secured the Old Vicarage's place in the nation's literary and cultural history. Even for Brooke, writing a century ago, it was already a dream, a poetic construct, but no less potent for that. 'The Old Vicarage, Grantchester' together with the war sonnet 'The Soldier' remain two of the greatest elegies to a lost England of the imagination.

CHAPTER FIVE

A Dream
of Beauty

John Betjeman at Farnborough

'I T IS SOMETHING REALLY TERRIBLE, this longing for England we get when we are away,' the British press attaché in Dublin observed in the midst of the Second World War. In a talk entitled 'Oh to be in England ...', broadcast on the BBC Home Service in 1943, he summed up what the country meant for him:

> I do not believe we are fighting for the privilege of living in a highly
> developed community of ants ... For me ... England stands for the
> Church of England, eccentric incumbents, oil-lit churches, Women's
> Institutes, modest village inns, arguments about cow parsley on the
> altar, the noise of mowing machines on Saturday afternoons, local
> newspapers, local auctions, the poetry of Tennyson, Crabbe, Hardy
> and Matthew Arnold ... leaning on gates and looking across fields...

This tender evocation by John Betjeman (1906–84) is a classic statement of the emotional lure of an England of rural parishes. The romantic vision rose before him, but it was a view from a distance, just as it had been for Rupert Brooke when he penned 'The Old Vicarage, Grantchester' in the Café des Westens in Berlin. Brooke's poem had immediately become a touchstone for ideas about national identity at a time of crisis. It provided a focus for an idealized past, an instantly recognizable place of safety in the shifting circumstances of the present. In the Second World War, just as in the First, this construct became a vital element of the iconography of national survival. Here was an England worth fighting and dying for.

This project of fixing the nation's identity (spiritual, cultural, literary), and finding a voice to express it, had been taken up by many writers and artists during the interwar years. Betjeman himself had rootled around ancient buildings since his prep school days in Oxford, as he recalled in his verse autobiography *Summoned by Bells* (1960): 'All that was crumbling, picturesque and quaint/Informed my taste', and in the 1930s he had collaborated with the artist John Piper to produce some of the famous Shell Guides. This was a literal and metaphysical mapping of a country that was felt to be disappearing, and at its core lay English parish life. It is not surprising, therefore, that Betjeman chose to make his home in one of the country's most beautiful rectories, the newly decommissioned Old Rectory at Farnborough.

The parish of Farnborough stands at the highest point on the Berkshire Downs, 720 feet above sea level. The winds blow unchecked across the great swathes of fields, with 'nothing between you and America', as the daughter of Farnborough's last rector put it. The village is approached via a single-lane track that winds up the hill from Wantage. Trees, planted for shelter, gallantly trying to fulfil their protective duties, surround the hamlet. At its centre is the tower of the twelfth-century church of All Saints, where Betjeman worshipped, read and was bell-ringer for the six years (1945–51) he lived in Farnborough.

Although the compilers of the *History of the County of Berkshire* (1924) dismisssed the village as consisting of 'a few brick cottages which are of little interest', these exacting historians did dedicate a paragraph to the rectory, a surprisingly elegant edifice for such a small parish, a reflection of the social status of the incumbents who for several hundred years were members of the Price family. These were gentlemen who attended the assizes at Abingdon in a coach and four in 1760, and whose standing required a certain graciousness in their surroundings. The clerical home they created for themselves presents itself as the perfect parsonage. Standing back from the road in beautifully laid out gardens, it is a house of exquisite scale and proportion, the embodiment of the rural peaceability that Betjeman evoked in his wartime broadcast on his vision of England.

The rectory was built in the mid-eighteenth century, the zenith of rectory building in England, and completed in 1749. The elegant, symmetrical façade of

The Old Rectory, Farnborough, by John Betjeman.

An Osbert Lancaster drawing of John Betjeman and friends singing 'Sumer is Icumen In' at a village concert in Uffington, 1935. The other performers are Maurice Bowra (standing next to Betjeman in the front), Lord Berners at the piano, Adrian Bishop, Cara Lancaster, Osbert Lancaster on the flute and Penelope Betjeman plucking the guitar on the table.

genteel and perfecting proportions presented an imposing vision to the passing parishioners, who were 'none but farmers'. In 1758 a fire consumed all the stables, barns, outhouses, hayricks, woodpiles and 'seven good horses' – a devastating loss of 'above £300' for the tenant – but the new rectory was untouched. Today, the fine bell cupola sits in perfect harmony with the red and black Berkshire brick front and the tiled roof. As an architectural addition, the cupola had a particular appeal to Betjeman, evidenced by the title of his verse autobiography, *Summoned by Bells*. The bell, which had called the end of the working day to generations of farm workers, was the summons for the Betjeman children to come in from the fields. It still rings for the odd high day and holiday. An elegant porch with fine Doric columns completes the frontage, the whole exuding balance and respectability. It is arguably the architectural expression of a reassuring picture of England's rural certainties.

John Betjeman and his wife, Penelope, bought Farnborough Rectory in 1945, moving there from a rented farmhouse in Uffington, a village nestling at the foot of the Berkshire Downs. There the couple had joined in wholeheartedly with socials in the village hall, playing darts in the local pub, bell-ringing and worshipping in the large church known as 'the Cathedral of the Vale'. 'Uffers' had worked well for the young couple following their marriage in 1933. The London commute to his job on the *Architectural Review* from Uffington station, still lit by oil lamps, was not arduous for Betjeman, and Penelope, a fine horse-woman, could hunt as often as she cared to on her beautiful grey, Moti (Hindi for 'pearl'), a gift from her doting father, the head of the Indian Army until 1935. They felt the exile from Uffers keenly in the years 1941–43 when Betjeman was posted in Ireland. 'We do miss not having any proper parish life,' Penelope had written to John and Myfanwy Piper.

Upon their return to England, the Betjemans' landlord at Uffington gave them notice and the search for a new home began. By now, with the addition of their two children, Paul and Candida, a larger house was required. A friend told them that the Old Rectory at Farnborough was on the market. 'John was absolutely potty about it and was determined to get it whatever happened,' Penelope recalled. 'It so happened that the day that the auction was to take place in the Town Hall, Wantage, coincided with VE Day when all the trains were "Sunday trains" and everything virtually came to a stop … John was in an absolute state.' The ever-resourceful Penelope drove to the auction from Uffington in her four-wheel pony cart and secured the house for £3,500. The couple possessed nothing like this sum, so Penelope's father, the Field Marshal, soon to be made Lord Chetwode, stepped in with a late wedding present of the required amount. Betjeman wrote to his friend Evelyn Waugh, who had his own gentleman's residence at Piers Court in Gloucestershire, announcing the purchase: 'Propeller's [Penelope's] father has just bought Farnborough Rectory, Nr Wantage for us: 1730-ish. Red brick seven hundred feet up on the downs. No water, no light, no heat. Beech trees all round.'

The spartan conditions inside the rectory appealed to the new incumbents. To the villagers' consternation the first thing Penelope did was to remove a bathroom (just as, at about the same time, the rector-poet R. S. Thomas removed the noisy and unappealing central heating from his rectory at Manafon to preserve the ascetic atmosphere). Mod-cons did not appeal to Betjeman, who was famously fond of uncleanliness, even contributing an article praising dirt to the magazine *Lilliput*. The pragmatic and aristocratic Penelope did not mind the lack of modern living conveniences either; there wasn't even a wireless with which to listen to Betjeman's famous broadcasts, so Penelope and her guests would decamp to a neighbour's cottage to hear him.

Water had to be fetched daily from the village pump (this was still the case in 1955 when the present owners took possession). There was no mains drainage either. After staying with the Betjemans during their first Christmas at Farnborough, Lord Chetwode pronounced it to be like 'living in the dark ages': the 'lav plugs don't pull and the bath water keeps running out'. The fact that his daughter had carved the ham at the wrong angle did not improve his temper. With no electricity, a gloomy form of lighting was provided by paraffin lamps. In the small, narrow lamp room (it still exists today) Betjeman undertook one of his few domestic duties, trimming the wicks before lighting the lamps. As in many rectories conceived and built by clerical architects long before central heating was dreamed of, the cold was all-pervasive and may explain why in so many Betjeman family memories domestic activity is centred around the kitchen, where there was a warm range, or in the inner hall, which had a similar, primitive heat source.

Despite the lack of creature comforts, for Penelope the first marital home that they owned was a 'dream of beauty', sitting in twelve acres including a wood and two fields. She recognized that it needed a lot of work, that it 'wasn't very attractive inside, it was just a very beautiful façade ... [John] said it was like buying a Cézanne, a beautiful picture.' The house itself she said was 'falling down

John, Candida, Paul and Penelope Betjeman with the Dalmatian, Peter Pudding,
in the garden at Farnborough in 1948, taken by Bassano.

and needs six servants'. It came with one *in situ*, the gardener, 'whose wages you had to pay, and I didn't think we were in that income group, quite honestly,' she wrote. 'It will probably kill us in the end.' On one level her premonition was correct: the Old Rectory was to witness the death of her marriage.

The previous incumbent, the Revd Puxley and his family, had had full domestic backup despite his modest living (he 'never earned more than £350 a year,' according to his daughter). This comparatively modest income notwithstanding, morning prayers in the rectory counted the four family members, Beulah North the cook, Abbot the gardener/chauffeur who lived in the lodge, a nanny and a parlour maid. Abbot remained a much-valued part of the household in the Betjemans' time and together with two sisters from the village, Florrie and Pearl, made up the somewhat diminished staff. An added bonus for Betjeman, who by his own admission was susceptible to the 'very direct stuff' of physical attraction, was the younger sister's obvious charms: 'Keep me from Thelma's sister Pearl!/She puts my senses in a whirl,' he wrote in the poem 'Agricultural Caress' (1966), changing just one of the names.

Penelope took charge of the cooking and even the fastidious Evelyn Waugh conceded the food was 'delicious'. The kitchen was, and still is, to the far right of the entrance hall. It was originally the village schoolroom and had a window looking onto the rectory lawn, a good vantage point from which to espy approaching visitors. All the family's meals were taken in here, never the dining room, where the table was usually covered in a mass of Betjeman's papers. Patrick Cullinan, the poet, stayed with the family when he was 17 and remembered 'a dark but friendly kitchen where we had our meals and … John opening and decanting the most delicious bottles of claret.' In the Puxley era, the annual choir supper had taken place in the kitchen, cooked on the capacious range by Beulah North. After this the choir (men and boys only), who were also the bell-ringers, would stagger over to the church to ring in the New Year.

The Puxley family seemed to have been living the rural parish dream during the 1930s when Betjeman and Piper were beginning to fix it poetically and pictorially. These were the days when the rector still rode out to see his parishioners in the fields; when the church was the centre of village life; when the surpliced choir still processed up and down the aisle making a joyful noise unto the Lord; when candlelit Evensong was, according to the Revd Puxley's daughter, Rosemary, 'thrilling'.

The war had intruded rudely on this idyll. The rector's daughter, who had danced on the lawn with a local farmer's son, left to join the Auxillary Territorial Service and never lived in the rectory again. The pale Doric columns by the entrance were painted dark brown in the belief that this would prevent them attracting enemy aircraft. Two years into the war the rector himself retired, lamenting in Betjeman-like terms the arrival of 'the weekender who spent his Sundays unsuitably dressed, washing his car and taking no interest in the village'.

According to Rosemary Puxley, the next rector stayed only 'ten minutes', and it was left to Betjeman to take up the legacy of the rectory. He fixed this receding rectorial dream forever in poems such as 'House of Rest' (1954), where, from the confines of her chair in a nursing home, the grey-eyed rector's wife is transported back

> To village church and village pond
> And ample rectory [...]

> Aroused at seven, to bed by ten,
> They fully lived each day,
> Dead sons, so motor-bike-mad then,
> And daughters far away.

'My experience is that there is no Faith in English villages at all, only convention,' Betjeman wrote to a friend in March 1950, 'but,' he added, 'that the convention can be turned into Faith.' This was the voice of a rector *manqué*. Initially the fit with rectory life was perfect for the couple. He was rector in all but name: bell-ringing, reading the lesson in church and generally providing a lead to the village were all 'duties' he took on with a kind of ecclesiastical seriousness. As he explained to Evelyn Waugh: 'If we were to desert it, there would be no one to whip up people to attend the services, to run the church organizations, to keep the dilatory and woolly-minded incumbent (who lives in another village) to the celebration of Communion services any Sunday.' And though he never had a seat on the council of the rural deanery, Betjeman took up his place as protector of the local churches through his long-term membership of the Oxfordshire Preservation Trust.

From his base at Farnborough Betjeman embarked upon more Shell Guides with John Piper, touring the counties of England ('ruin-crawling', as

Penelope and John Betjeman in clerical mode for his part in his
Oxford friend John Sutro's film *The Sailor's Return*, 1935.

Piper put it) when petrol rations allowed, writing up descriptions of churches as well as composing his poetry. For Betjeman, church-crawling 'introduces you to the history of England in stone and wood and glass which is always truer than what you read in books'. Here were the tangible signs of eternal verities. The theme would be taken up by Philip Larkin, who later told Betjeman of his own forays into the countryside around Hull by bicycle on Sundays. These solitary outings were punctuated by stops at empty churches where he would wander in, removing his bicycle clips in 'awkward reverence'. As he wrote in 'Church Going' (1954), they were places 'not worth stopping for. / Yet stop I did'.

In the rectory itself, Betjeman, dismissive of interior decorators, took charge of most of the arrangements, transforming a Georgian interior into a Victorian one. The climbing ivy wallpaper in the main bedroom was from Green & Abbot, and Candida remembers a blue art nouveau design was chosen for his dressing room and a reddish Gilbert Scott pattern for the dining room, where he spent the mornings dictating. This Victorian aesthetic was also very pronounced in his choice of art: the many paintings by his friend John Piper aside, there were works by Dante Gabriel Rossetti, William Holman Hunt, Myles Birket Foster and Lawrence Alma-Tadema. According to his daughter, Betjeman never spent more than £15 on a picture.

There was one 'Indian' bedroom decorated to Penelope's taste and hung with thirty aquatints of India, a nod to Penelope's childhood home as well as to her academic interest in all things Indian. This was the room used by Betjeman's secretary, Miss Webb. She helped with his architectural books, dictation, the cataloguing of information for his *Collins Guide to English Parish Churches* (published in 1958), and was adept at piecing together her employer's poems from scraps of paper randomly produced from his capacious pockets.

There was much laughter in the rectory. A practical joker, Betjeman kept a stuffed crocodile hidden in a shrubbery to startle guests, and he was also a charismatic master of ceremonies for the post-Sunday service treasure hunt for local children held in the rectory garden. He joyfully continued the village tradition of dances on the lawn, for which Abbot the gardener hung hundreds of fairy lights in the surrounding trees, casting a magical glow over the evening just as Rosemary Puxley remembered similar occasions during the 1930s.

The golden aura of childhood permeates the Betjeman children's memories, too. Up on the attic floor they inhabited a fairy-tale world that included their father's treasured teddy bear Archie, the eponymous hero of his children's book *Archie and the Strict Baptists* (1977), who was stored in one of the bedroom cupboards. From her bedroom window, tucked behind 'Archie's parapet', Candida could survey the Berkshire Downs, which seemed to melt into an infinite horizon, and she believed that the whole world was laid out before her. Even the names of the ancient villages were incantatory and mysterious, connecting her to another, primeval world.

'Farnborough was my favourite place on earth. I seemed to have complete freedom,' Candida recalled. In her memory, the rectory represents a world of fun and innocence. Unlike the Tennysons, the Brontës and Dorothy L. Sayers, the Betjeman children were not inhabitants of an isolated working rectory with its inherent tensions. Farnborough was already the 'old rectory' and in democratic postwar Britain the children of the gentleman incumbent were not separated from the local children by status or education. They attended the same village school as them, at least until prep-school age, when educational tradition intervened; Paul was then sent off to the Dragon School in Oxford, like his father before him.

As the rural rectors of old, Betjeman often retreated to his book-lined study on the first floor where, overlooking the lawn and the ancient thatched tithe barn, he would spend the afternoons writing poetry or working on his reviews, books piled up in leaning towers around him. The room was painted cornflower blue, and, although a window had been added in Edwardian times, it was always dark. The children remember being allowed to enter this hallowed space in the evenings and how they were taught to handle their father's precious books with due reverence. For Betjeman, old books were another tangible link with the past. In the faded cream colour of a particular precious tome he could 'smell the England that has gone: a slightly musty smell, which all old books have, and which makes me think of the golden leather backs of the rows of shelves in a country-house library, of the deep silence of the fields outside ...' In the right-hand drawer of the desk he kept a glass case in which was preserved a large centipede and a cardboard souvenir that opened out into the recognizable shape of the Crystal Palace; both were objects of fascination for the children.

At first, the role of 'rector's wife' was taken up by Penelope with gusto. As the daughter of the former British commander-in-chief in India she was a natural fit for running the Farnborough Women's Institute. She also ran the socials in the village hall and helped organize the village refreshment rotas for the fortnightly whist drives. Miss Dearlove, the harmonium player from the

Puxleys' time, played the piano, accompanied by the band members from nearby Ardington, who together concluded these evenings with a resounding hokey cokey.

Penelope also took her place in the flower rota, decorating the church at harvest festival and encouraging the village children to collect and press wild flowers and learn their Latin names. Her husband sponsored the annual prize for this hobby, awarding a copy of *The Observer's Book of British Wild Flowers* to the child with the most impressive collection.

These were the years of postwar austerity and the lack of water, heating and light at the old rectory was not unusual in rural areas, although Betjeman railed at what he called the 'Slave State' created by Labour government, which he blamed for keeping them in these primitive conditions. The cold was such that Evelyn Waugh reckoned both Betjeman and Penelope 'put on Jaeger combinations on the 1st of September and keep them on for all purposes until the 2nd week of May'. The ever practical Penelope found ways to supplement the severity of the ration book through her resourceful husbandry. The rectory's smallholding supplied vital provisions, just as it had for many previous incumbents. Livestock included two 'housecows', Buttercup and Daisy, whose milk was churned into dark yellow salty butter, a treat not entirely to the taste of the Betjeman children. Penelope had plans to make it profitable too, which would enable Betjeman to give up his bread-and-butter reviewing and spend more time writing poems and topographical books. However, the small farm was never a financial success. It took up much of Penelope's time and energy (it was, said her husband, 'jungle work'), and her children remember her outside the rectory 'doing things with animals most of the time'.

The domain outside the house was where she seemed most at home, and although Betjeman himself claimed an aversion to them, Penelope made sure that horses were central to Farnborough life. Tulira, the Connemara grey, was often hitched up to the dogcart or trolley and driven by Penelope at breakneck speed along the Ridgeway. Candida remembers clerics and Wantage nuns, as well as Father Nash, the incumbent for West Ilsley and Farnborough, being ordered into the trolley cart by her redoubtable mother, with the odd casualty as they flew over the bumpy track. Penelope often drove standing up like a latter-day Boudicca, balanced by the reins, children on cushions and rugs in the back, some sitting on the end of the cart with their legs dangling down.

Part of the White Horse at Uffington on the Berkshire Downs, photographed by Edwin Smith.

Hunter trials and gymkhanas permeated their existence. Mrs Glover ran the local events and a young woman called Diana Russell usually won everything. These occasions were perfect fodder for Betjeman, standing on the sidelines watching, ever the acute social observer, as evident in 'Hunter Trials'. (1954):

It's awf'lly bad luck on Diana,
    Her ponies have swallowed their bits;
She fished down their throats with a spanner
    And frightened them all into fits.

Inside the rectory the smell of tack wafted through the house along with the smoke from Betjeman's Passing Cloud cigarettes. As was her way in all her homes, Penelope brought the outside in at Farnborough. 'A horse sleeps in the kitchen,' Waugh told Nancy Mitford. 'Harness everywhere,' he added in his diary. Surrounded by the smells and sights of the indoor stable, the children would gather around the stove to hear Betjeman's ghost stories, thrilled and terrified by tales such as 'Seeking Whom He May Devour', a ghastly tale set in a gloomy church in the Lincolnshire Fens. He loved reading aloud, as his father had read to him, and was particularly fond of all the M. R. James ghost stories, one of which was enacted for the village in the rectory hall. 'Apart from the kitchen, the hall seemed to be the only place we ever sat,' Candida recalled. 'The dining room, which we never used anyway, had been taken over by Miss Webb and her typewriter and the sitting room was cold and no one EVER went in there.'

The convivial Betjemans were popular and generous hosts and had a vast array of friends and acquaintances beating their way to the rectory's ever-open door. Among the most frequent visitors were the Pipers and the Osbert Lancasters. After meals in the kitchen accompanied by a generous supply of Betjeman's fine decanted claret, the assembled company would move to the hall where the entertainment continued. Along with indiviudal performances of music-hall songs, the whole company joined in with raucous renditions of Theo Marzials numbers, which rang through the rectory.

Evelyn Waugh was also a frequent guest, despite his disparaging views of the house, which he described as lightless, stuffy, cold and pokey. 'How very Evelyn to write so readably and inaccurately,' was Betjeman's comment later.

Paul and Penelope outside the Old Rectory, Farnborough.

Tulira pulling the trolley cart loaded with John Betjeman, family, friends and villagers.

John Betjeman in 1949, photographed by John Gay.

When Waugh was in residence, passionate and unsettling doctrinal discussions became increasingly common, taking the place of the more convivial musical entertainment. Waugh shared with Betjeman an elegiac attitude to the old world order. In *A Handful of Dust* (1934) he explored the moral unravelling of a nation's culture, but where Betjeman and Piper sought active ways to shore it up, Waugh retreated from it into Catholicism and his own isolated life, first at Piers Court in Gloucestershire and then at Combe Florey in Somerset, the same parish that earlier was home to the ebullient and profoundly humane rector Sydney Smith after he had left Foston. Unlike Betjeman, Waugh kept his distance from involvement in the parish and from the Church of England itself, criticising his High Anglican friend in the most strident terms: 'Now I find you expounding Protestant devotional practices from the pulpit. This WILL NOT DO.'

Betjeman was fighting a rearguard action in the parish as well as in his poetry, and in his correspondence with the hectoring Waugh, a crusading Catholic convert. Continually forced to defend his position as an Anglican, over the years his weariness becomes palpable: 'Religion first. Believe me I find it no pleasure. Indeed to worship here at Farnborough requires a great act of Faith … the only bulwark against complete paganism is the church and its chief supporters are Propellor and me.' Waugh's acerbic response was to continue his verbal barrage on all fronts: 'It would be a pity to go to HELL because you prefer Henry Moore to Michelangelo. THIS GOES FOR PENELOPE TOO.'

Cracks began to appear in the perfect façade of life at Farnborough. The architectural harmony of the rectory's exterior was not matched by the state of the Betjemans' domestic life inside. Penelope, often alone with the farm and the children while Betjeman was in London, turned to Rome in her isolation. This was not a direct result of Waugh's bullying – Catholicism had held a strong appeal for her since the early 1930s – but after a difficult year of 'great strain and tension' for both, Penelope converted in 1948. Although Farnborough life would continue until 1951, there was now a chasm between the couple that could not be bridged. A profound part of their relationship had been based on mutual faith and worship. Betjeman now felt alone, writing in 'The Empty Pew' of the depths of his sense of abandonment by the woman who is 'Still half my life' as he sits in the church 'present with our Church of England few', glancing across at that 'deserted pew'. The poem concludes with the poignant lines: 'In the Perspective of Eternity/The pain is nothing – but, ah God, in Time.'

Betjeman's agony, however, was deemed 'too personal' by his publisher Jock Murray, who excluded the poem from *A Few Late Chrysanthemums* (1954).

'I had thought that however much Penelope and I quarrelled, at any rate the Church stayed the same – rather like old Archie, something you can always turn to,' Betjeman wrote. 'And Penelope was really very Anglican by temperament – the sort of person who always quarrels with the vicar.' But previous certainties were no longer reliable. Although Betjeman was as hospitable as ever, the charm of the house's spartan aesthetic was beginning to pall for visitors. A bitter tone creeps into Betjeman's correspondence, as in a letter of 8 March 1950 to Patrick Cullinan: 'You who have always lived in luxury may be horrified by the squalor, the lateness of meals (eaten in the kitchen), the noise of children, the smells of cooking, the dullness of the surrounding scenery, and my early morning nervous irritability?' Breakfasts had become increasingly tetchy affairs as Betjeman's liverish temper involved him railing at marmalade on his cuffs and 'lost' newspapers, which he was usually sitting on.

The romance of the place that had so charmed him at the beginning was being replaced by premonitions of disease and mortality. 'This village is full of tragedy as usual,' he wrote to a friend in 1949. 'A case of ill-treatment of children in a house opposite, yet not such as one can put the NSPCC on to it. Another case of a farm worker with a young family condemned to death by cancer.' In addition, the landscape that was of such sacred importance to him was being eaten away before his eyes, as he had written in 'The Plantster's Vision' (1945):

I have a Vision of The Future, chum,
The workers' flats in fields of soya beans
Tower up like silver pencils, score on score:

To make matters worse, in 1946 the Atomic Energy Research Establishment was established at Harwell, outside Wantage, and ugly prefabs for the workers sprang up around the parish. 'Why do you need to cover the downs with prefabs?' he stormed at the AERE's first director, the atomic physicist and Nobel Prize winner Sir John Cockcroft, and in 'The Dear Old Village' (1954) bemoaned that:

Nature is out of date and GOD is too;
Think what atomic energy can do!'

John Piper's memorial window to John Betjeman, All Saints, Farnborough, 1986.

The threat was not confined to a distant landscape, but encroaching on Farnborough's immediate environs. The ancient, cathedral-like tithe barn that had stood for several hundred years at the edge of the rectory lawn was demolished. 'It was a bit like pulling down a church,' Betjeman mourned. He had always responded to the voicefulness of such buildings, to their moral architecture and history of civility – the 'centuries of texture' – with far more than academic interest. From his early role as assistant editor of the *Architectural Review*, he had viewed the parochial and rural buildings of England as the building blocks of the nation's spiritual and cultural life. The barn, like his own rectory, was modest compared to the great cathedrals, but both had survived periods of political and religious upheaval and two world wars. They did this by holding mutability and continuity in balance. For Betjeman, the destruction of the barn signified an assault on the most esteemed values of Englishness. 'It changed the feeling of the place,' Candida remembered. 'My dad minded because he loved the barn. He said it was a noble building, and it had hurt him to see it destroyed.'

From his desk in the study the view of the ancient church and graveyard remained, but the picture around it was changing irrevocably. When the elm trees in the churchyard were felled another layer of protection had gone, leaving the church, now in the hands of the over-zealous Revd Nash (the reluctant traveller in Penelope's cart), exposed. There was no longer any 'mystery, no hiding in the shade,' as Betjeman lamented. He minded terribly; the physical collapse of the barn and the trees brought into focus the domestic and moral collapse inside the rectory. There were echoes of the poem that had so influenced his childhood, Oliver Goldsmith's *The Deserted Village* (1770), where the destruction of an ancient village and farms to make way for a rich man's landscaped park signals the loss of the connective tissue between a land and its people.

Christmas that last year, 1950, was a dislocated affair. The cat, Fritz, who had been with them since Uffington, was found dead behind the boiler on Boxing Day. They had been presented with an exorbitant estimate to run electricity down the drive, and Betjeman felt he had 'run out of steam'. He made a desultory attempt at escape by renting Kelmscott Manor, near Lechlade, where William Morris had lived, but he never moved in. Like the Speckleby rector in 'A Lincolnshire Tale' (1945), his home was metaphorically crumbling around him:

The mansion was ruined, the empty demesne
Was slowly reverting to marshland again –
Marsh where the village was, grass in the Hall,
And the church and the Rectory waiting to fall.

The spell cast by Farnborough, his safe architectural and spiritual anchorage, had been broken. The rift in the marriage, the expense of living in a comparatively grand house whose upkeep was beyond them, and the strains of isolated village life on an essentially urban and urbane temperament had all taken their toll. They decided to sell the rectory and move five miles to 'alien territory in red-brick Wantage'. At his desk in the rectory in June 1951, Betjeman took up his pen one last time to write to Patrick Cullinan:

> I write this to you at three p.m. while the above [The Old Rectory]
> is being auctioned down the hill at the Bear Hotel, Wantage. We have
> put a reserve of eight and a half thousand on it and I don't think it'll
> reach the reserve. But the woodlice still walk on the landing here
> unperturbed. And what am I more than a woodlouse?'

As it turned out, the house was sold for £11,000, a handsome profit, but it was in all other ways a loss. Stanley Baldwin, the Conservative politican, had famously stated in a speech in 1931 that the locus of the nation's spiritual and cultural core was to be found in the country; here lay 'the eternal values and the eternal traditions from which we must never allow ourselves to be separated'. At Farnborough, Betjeman had hoped to make a reality of the rural dream in a rectory and parish that for him were enduring symbols of cultural survival. But the Betjemans' married life was disintegrating just as the postwar nation was becoming increasingly distanced from Baldwin's 'eternal values and the eternal traditions'. The rectory, like so many other parochial buildings at this time of the great sell-off by the Church Commissioners, was just another property on the market.

Betjeman became an increasingly popular national figure and was appointed Poet Laureate in 1972. Through his radio and television broadcasts he guided the nation to reappraise its parochial buildings as well as leading campaigns to preserve great Victorian structures, such as the one fronting London's St Pancras station. In the face of what he saw as 'as society's new loneliness, new restlessness' parish life and church architecture provided much-needed cultural and spiritual anchors. The parish church continued to be at the heart of this sustaining vision. His friend Philip Larkin shared his view (despite being an agnostic) and articulated it in 'Church Going':

> For, though I've no idea
> What this accoutred frowsty barn is worth,
> It pleases me to stand in silence here;
>
> A serious house on serious earth it is,
> In whose blent air all our compulsions meet,
> Are recognized, and robed as destinies.

They shared 'a passion for churches', the title Betjeman gave to a 1974 television programme on this, the core of his vision:

> And though for Church
> We may not seem to care,
> It's deeply part of us.
> Thank God it's there.

In his last years Betjeman suffered from Parkinson's disease and he died at his home in Trebetherick, Cornwall, in May 1984. He is buried there in the churchyard of his beloved parish church of St Enodoc.

CHAPTER SIX

The Deep Peace of Wild Places

R. S. Thomas at Manafon

I N 1942, AT THE NADIR OF THE SECOND WORLD WAR, R. S. Thomas (1913–2000) and his wife, Elsi, motored up a long, tree-lined drive in an Austin 7 with their goat in the back. This ensemble was distinctly at odds with the handsome Georgian rectory that stood at the end of the drive, guarded by ancient yew trees. Indeed, Manafon Rectory, the first of poet-rector R. S. Thomas's three rural parish houses, is a surprisingly grand affair – a well-appointed gentleman's residence refurbished under the terms of Gilbert's Act of 1776 – in Montgomeryshire in the Welsh borders. Square, solid, balanced, the architecture perfectly encapsulates the moral dimension of its function as an outpost of the Church in Wales. In addition to its eleven bedrooms and three bathrooms, it once boasted stables, a coach house and paddocks, the necessary accoutrements for an eighteenth-century gentleman cleric.

In every respect, this gracious house was a long way from Cardiff, where R. S. Thomas had been born, the only son of a merchant seaman and a powerful, aspirational mother who steered her boy towards the respectable vocation of the Church as a way out of the port city and up the social scale. A childhood move to Anglesey introduced him to the wonders of the natural world, a landscape that he never left imaginatively, and one that he would return to, ending his days as an old man on the Llŷn peninsula; the final point on what he described in his autobiography *Neb* (1985) as his 'oval' journey. Restless in the landlocked parishes of Chirk and Manafon and the socially claustrophobic (for him) Eglwys-fach in Ceredigion, his was the outsider's long journey to find a 'home'.

Following a degree in classics at the University College of North Wales in Bangor, where he became known as R.S. while playing rugby (to distinguish him from the other Thomases in the team), he trained for the priesthood and was ordained in 1937. His first curacy at Chirk came to an end in 1940 when he married the artist and illustrator Elsi Eldridge, who had been teaching art at nearby Oswestry; the vicar did not want a married curate. The couple moved to Tallarn Green in Maelor Saesneg, near Wrexham, but R.S. was never happy there; he felt stranded. It was too English and he was intent on establishing and nurturing his Welsh poetic voice. As he recalled later in the essay 'Y llwybrau gynt' / 'The Paths Gone By' (1972), 'in the evening I could see the Welsh hills some fifteen miles away, magical and mysterious as ever. I realized what I had done. My place was not here on this plain amongst these Welsh with English accents and attitudes. I set about learning Welsh, so as to get back to the real Wales of my imagination.' So in 1942, when the opportunity to move to Manafon presented itself, he readily accepted this tiny – and to him more remote – parish of hill farms, where he was to be the incumbent until 1954.

The village, such as it is, lies in a small valley some five hundred feet above sea level, with hills rising up to nearly a thousand feet enclosing it in a harsh embrace. R.S. describes it in *Neb* as a place that barely exists: 'no village, there, only a church, a school, a public house and a shop.' Eric Jones, R.S.'s nearest neighbour, whose family farmed 120 acres up the hillside from Manafon Rectory, remarked that 'the village is set in the strangest landscape'. It does indeed have a feeling of otherworldliness, its past peppered with stories that emphasize its liminal, misty atmosphere. Local legend has it that the poet and agricultural economist Gwallter Mechain, who held the living in the early nineteenth century, was a wizard who cast spells on his parishioners. It was in Manafon churchyard in 1878 that the first cremated body was buried in consecrated ground in Britain – apparently on the instructions of a determined and morbidly curious Manafon heiress who had the body of one Harry Crookenden exhumed from Brompton Cemetery, transported to Italy for cremation (illegal in Britain at that time), then shipped back to Montgomeryshire. This was the mystical background to R.S.'s first Welsh parish; rooted in the past, 'Brittle with relics', 'sham ghosts' and an awareness of 'the spilled blood / That went to the making of the wild sky' ('Welsh Landscape', 1952).

When Elsi climbed out of the car with her goat, she was immediately struck by the isolation. 'No one passes through Manafon on their way to

The rectory at Manafon. A Georgian gentleman-rector's residence, to R.S. Thomas it was 'The white house in the cool grass/Membraned with shadow' ('The Return', 1955).

R. S. Thomas, 1945, by his wife, M. E. Eldridge. Elsi was already an established artist when the couple married in 1940.

anywhere,' she commented later in her unpublished memoir, rather forlornly. Four years older than R.S., Elsi was discovering that her life as a rector's wife was in stark contrast to her upbringing in Wimbledon as a member of a gregarious and well-to-do family. Her father was a jeweller. She was well travelled, having spent time in Paris staying with the family of a fur dealer to improve her French, and as a student at the Royal College of Art she had won the Prix de Rome travelling scholarship, visiting the connoisseur Bernard Berenson at the Villa I Tatti outside Florence. By the time Elsi met R.S., she had already enjoyed considerable artistic success and exhibited at the Royal Academy. Now, in this marriage of seeming opposites, she was being led away from everything that she had previously known and valued. It would be a journey into the wild, like that of the Sayers family moving from Oxford to a remote Fenland parish, Elsi dutifully following R.S. as he led her patriarchally deeper and deeper into Wales. 'And so it came to pass,' he intoned with Old Testament resonance, adding: 'I wouldn't want to go as far as being shut up with my own excreta in some little place in the Egyptian desert, but Jesus himself did withdraw into the wilderness.'

The young rector and his wife entered their new home through the porch, with its nineteenth-century wrought-iron scrollwork, and thence to the panelled hall where Elsi would later place her collection of little Chinese junks and animal skulls on the mantelpiece. R.S. ascended the stairs, and from there stood to look through the window 'across the river to the field on the other side of it and up to the bare ridge where the clouds were hurrying by'. This was the seclusion he had sought, the landscape in which to find his poetic voice, and yet he immediately sensed a form of entrapment. 'That very moment he foresaw the seasons before him,' he wrote in *Neb*, 'with the weather turning from rain to shine and from heat to snow … There was nothing else to see but the land and the sky under the changing seasons.'

In *Neb* R.S. cited Edward Thomas's poem 'The New House' (1915) to describe his sense of dislocation on arrival at the rectory. He found himself occupying a small place in a continuous narrative over which he had little control: 'All was foretold me; naught / Could I foresee;' Edward Thomas wrote – a feeling that resonated with R.S. Solace is offered in an articulation of the wildness of the natural world in which a still, small voice may be discerned – 'But I learnt how the wind would sound / After these things should be' the poem concludes. It is an austere consolation. R.S. recognized similar aspects in his own sensibility and surroundings. At Manafon he transposed the bleakness of the Welsh landscape and its people into his poetry of exile and struggle, where despite the hostile terrain, flashes of divinity and human nobility are occasionally glimpsed through the veil of primeval darkness.

R.S. was saved from the prospect of unremitting climatic and seasonal monotony by the presence of the river Rhiw, which runs past the back of the rectory and through the valley on its way to join the Severn six miles to the east. Here was change, unpredictability, interest, 'a living thing and as full of moods as a girl,' he wrote in *Neb*. In summer this capricious river all but dried up, but in the autumn and winter, after the rains, it would suddenly swell and sweep into the cellars that ran under part of the house, an event that R.S. recounted in familiar biblical terms: 'He then opened the door and, behold, the water was within a foot of the head of the steps!'

When R.S. and Elsi arrived, the parish consisted mostly of hill farmers and their families eking out an existence, battered by the extremities of wet and windy weather. Machinery had not yet made its mark on the farming communities of mid-Wales, and at Manafon tractors were still unknown. The men worked with their hands, hoeing, shearing, gathering hay and cutting the hedges. R.S. stood apart, with, as he put it in *Neb*, 'the mark of the church and the library' upon him, slightly mystified, wondering what was in the minds of these solitary beings in the field hoeing or docking swedes, hour after hour. It was a far tougher, more elemental world than he had anticipated, a long way from the lyrical dream he had been nursing: 'I had seen this track of country from the train at dusk through romantic spectacles,' he later reflected. 'I now found myself amongst tough, materialistic hard-working people, who measured one another by the acre and by the pound.'

While the farmers farmed, their rector strode up and down the hillsides, an angry Moses seeking revelation from above. R.S. was regarded with suspicion, the default response to strangers from those who inhabit such inhospitable terrain. For the Anglican parish priest, the real uphill climb was to find his position amid the strong Chapel presence. R.S. would chide his parishioners for their poor attendance. After only four children appeared at Sunday school in December 1944, he warned apocalyptically in the parish magazine: 'Parents of Manafon, for the last time I appeal to you.' The Christmas service of that year attracted a congregation of eleven. Those who did turn up more regularly would often fall asleep during the sermon, having had to walk

R. S. Thomas and his wife, Elsi, *c.* 1940, shortly after their marriage.

St Michael's Church, Manafon. 'It stands yet,' wrote R. S. Thomas, despite single-figure congregations and a strong Chapel presence in the parish.

considerable distances from their farms in order to attend. R.S. wrote of how he felt about his parishioners in 'A Priest to His People' (1946):

> Men of the hills, wantoners, men of Wales,
> With your sheep and your pigs and your ponies, your sweaty females,
> How I have hated you for your irreverence

And yet this was not the full story as he also saw in these 'men of the hills' qualities of resilience and dignity. It was this difficult engagement, rooted partly in respect and partly in distaste, which inspired R. S. Thomas's first published poetry. 'The strongly charactered hardness of these border people really did make an impression on me, as far as poetic material was concerned,' he later acknowledged. They were, he wrote unsparingly in 'Welsh Landscape', 'an impotent people, / Sick with inbreeding'. It was perhaps just as well that not many outsiders found their way there. When R.S. told people in the world beyond the name of the village, the response was always the same: 'Manafon? Where is it?'

For Elsi, however, Manafon and, in particular, the rectory garden, became a 'golden space', as Grantchester had been for Rupert Brooke. The valley was a haven for wildlife, teeming with house martins, long-tailed tits, swallows and owls, and there were trout in the river. In winter, the sun did not reach down into the valley until late morning and was gone by mid-afternoon, but the days of summer were halcyon, with a garden burgeoning with scented flowers, harebells, columbine and roses. 'It seemed like Paradise,' Elsi wrote in her memoirs. 'The apple orchard beside the river was full to the brim with white Poet's Eye narcissus, Red squirrels in the trees. The river only a short path's length from the back door of the kitchen ... Living there was like living in the middle of a lovely field. The grass billowing up to the door.' With stones from the river she built a wall and grew gentian and other alpines – 'Her care/ For green life has enabled/The weak things to grow', as R.S. wrote in 'The Untamed' (1963). She gloried in the rectory's old roses, including the magnificently scented 'Gloire de Dijon' and the yellow *Rosa banksiae* over the front door, whose fragrance pervaded the house in early summer. In the autumn there were 'showers of golden and brown leaves'.

R.S. helped out here and there, especially in the kitchen garden. When their son Gwydion was born in 1945 R.S. planted a larch tree at the front of the rectory, where it still stands. But R.S. was only playing in the half-truth of the 'tamed' gentleness of Elsi's garden. His chosen habitat was the 'wild/Sea of the grass' beyond, in the 'deep peace/Of wild places', as he wrote in 'The Untamed'.

Weather permitting, the afternoons were spent outside, Elsi gardening while her husband was stalking the hillsides. As he grew up, Gwydion played in the hay and made dens in empty pigsties. For him, as he described in a BBC interview, the rectory was 'a jewel of a house in the long grass by the river. Tall Abies nobilis fir trees, high yew hedges, an orchard, a kitchen garden, a cobbled courtyard, outhouses and secret rooms' provided a perfect setting for a curious child. 'He could explore the fields with curlews calling all round him,' Elsi remembered in her memoirs. 'One day he came running from the fields with a curlew's egg in his hand, such a large egg. He was able to show me, two fields away, the exact spot where he had found it, so that we were able to put it back in the nest.' Gwydion grew to understand and love the natural world. There he felt at home, soon learned to identify the highly poisonous black byrony berries and how to find the hiding places of various nuts and mushrooms, fungi and rare spindletree berries, a skill that usually secured the first prize for his display of autumn fruits in the annual local berries show. Even when it rained there was endless entertainment, the puddles in the gravel at the front of the rectory providing ideal circuits and obstacles for his Dinky Toys.

Elsi nursed her garden into a kind of Eden. But for R.S. the scene was anything but heavenly. For him, the long grass was not so much a backdrop of billowing pastoral softness as a constant threat whose advances he battled to keep at bay, both in the garden and in the nearby churchyard, the grass 'creeping perpetually nearer/This last outpost of time past' as he wrote in 'The Village' (1955). Scythe in hand, he kept up his counterattack against the 'long erosion of the green tide' – ineffectually as it turned out, for his scythe was often blunt. Not being a practical man he could never sharpen it properly so that, as his son recounted, 'there was a time in his life when for him mankind was divided into two species, those who could set an edge on a scythe and those who couldn't.'

'As the shadows grew longer,' Elsi noted in her memoirs, 'we were sad for we should have to go back into the house quite soon.' Inside, the gentle pastoral spell was broken. For R.S., austerity was a chosen aesthetic and a way of life. He writes about 'The simple house' and 'the strict palate' in 'Anniversary' (1961), echoing George Herbert's monastic precepts for the home of the parish priest; R.S. had edited a selection of Herbert's poetry in 1967 for Faber & Faber.

This austerity was a feature of all three of R.S.'s main homes, first practised at Manafon where there were no carpets, no wallpaper, few paintings on the walls (despite Elsi being an artist). Gwydion remembers it 'was beautiful but it was very cold'. With no electricity and no gas, open fires provided the only warmth and lighting came from the Aladdin lamps with their beautiful filigree wicks that were always breaking. In the winter, especially during the famous Arctic conditions of 1947 when the temperature was below freezing for considerable periods, there was frost on the inside of the windowpanes. Elsi tried, in vain, to keep out the cold by hanging long woollen blankets at the windows (or, in the bedrooms upstairs, variously coloured towels). Her husband either did not notice or preferred it that way; Gwydion remembers him in front of one of the open fires, his holey, threadbare socks discarded, painting his chilblains with iodine. 'My father reckoned minus eighteen was quite normal in winter.'

The water supply at the rectory came from an old well, shared with the sheep on a nearby hill, travelling through old pipes that R.S. spent all day trying to thaw with an oil lamp before they froze again at night. They would burst continually. When Elsi once had the water tested by the local chemist and called in for the results, he observed wryly, 'Well, you're not dead yet are you?'

Not much housework was done at Manafon. To Gwydion, sitting on the floor as his father fed him poached egg on toast under the table, the layers of dust were easily discernible. Elsi had little time and no money for the niceties of being houseproud. There was no vacuum cleaner, although on one occasion at Eglwys-fach, their next parish, a Goblin model was ordered and arrived at Glandyfi station where it stayed in its box for about a week until somebody went and picked it up. The box was opened and its contents examined with curiosity. Extraordinary looking and metallic green, the appliance made a noise like a force ten gale. 'My father turned it off,' Gwydion recalls. '"I don't think we need anything that makes a noise like that," he said, and threw it away.' There was no fridge and no washing machine.

R.S.'s obsession with routine meant that meals were subject to precision timing. Breakfast was taken at eight o'clock in the slate-floored kitchen as the trio thawed out by the Rayburn, particularly in the winter months. There was bread and cheese for R.S. at eleven, lunch at one in the dining room. Elsi cooked in the spartan kitchen on a paraffin stove, and like much else at Manafon this meal tended to be regimented and unvarying. Lamb, unsurprisingly, featured

Elsi and Gwydion by the river Rhiw, *c*. 1947.

Gwydion and R. S. Thomas in the garden of the rectory, Manafon, *c.* 1948.

heavily: a leg for Sunday lunch, with runner beans or peas when fresh, tinned vegetables if not, boiled potatoes, and tinned fruit with custard for pudding; Monday, leftovers, cold; Tuesday, the same but warmed up in gravy. The lamb reappeared as rissoles on Wednesday. Thursday, Gwydion remembers, was 'a peculiar pie' that seemed to contain eggs, tinned tomatoes and white sauce. Friday, there was plaice. If a rabbit had been sent in, there would be rabbit pie on Saturday, a red-letter day. If not, they would have to eat the stringy lamb's liver the butcher had supplied with the previous Sunday's joint. This was postwar cooking, and it was perfectly suited to the rector's doctrine of a 'strict palate'.

R.S. relaxed the rules a little for tea, his favourite meal, which he took at five o'clock. It was a hearty affair, reward for the afternoon spent in the garden scything or stomping the hillsides, consisting of several slices of bread and butter and jam, malt bread or bara brith, iced buns or a slice of Elsi's cake, and was the one feature of life exempted from austerity measures. R.S. did not drink tea although Elsi did, sitting in silence opposite him pouring hers from her little silver teapot, a vestige of more civilized times when she was a celebrated London artist with an open-topped Bentley in the drive. Supper at Manafon was at eight and, like lunch, served in the dusty dining room watched over by two Portuguese ceramic chickens perched on the dresser. This was the pattern for fifty years, Elsi providing meals like clockwork and taking care of the domestic side of life so that her husband could pursue his vocation as priest and poet unencumbered by petty concerns.

From 1950, Elsi taught evening classes for the extramural department of the University of Wales in Aberystwyth to supplement the family income. On these occasions R.S. was left in charge of the young Gwydion. The supper he would produce consisted of a piece of cheese, 'mould not unknown, Caerphilly usually', and a jar of pickled beetroot, presented on one of the rectory's bright blue plates, with yellow ivory-handled cutlery, all of which, according to Gwydion 'did not improve the food's appearance'.

In the kitchen, Elsi would bottle endlessly, utilizing everything she could from the productive kitchen garden and beyond. There were raspberries and blackberries for making jam, dandelions for dandelion wine, nettles for nettle beer. Eggs, milk and butter were supplied from the neighbouring farms, and she would bake cakes to take with her when she went to call on the Manafon parishioners, as well as those she made for the rector. The Rayburn never gave off enough heat to dispel the ever present chill; Gwydion was struck by the warmth of the hill farmers' kitchens where the steaming family washing and fitches of ham hung from the ceiling and the smell of freshly baked bread pervaded the air, a cosy alternative to the austere existence down at the rectory.

Despite the testing conditions, the kitchen did offer Elsi a form of refuge. Like the garden, it was her domain, and she did much to conjoin these two aspects of life at Manafon. Under her kitchen window she nurtured baby robins nesting in a tub of polyanthus, and when 'a horrible group of farmers came across the river with staves and sticks & shouting horribly' she threw open the kitchen door to shelter the 'very lovely' red fox who crept into a corner of the slate-floored dairy until the hunting party had moved on. In winter when she sat in front of the fire in the long room at the top of the kitchen stairs two harvest mice would climb onto her knee to share the warmth. The garden also entered the house via the run-down Victorian conservatory, a large unheated room that smelled to Gwydion like the Palm House at Kew. The floor had iron gratings and red tiles, and the paintwork, like much else at Manafon, was old and peeling, a layer of ochre visible through the bubbling navy blue on top. Here the Manafon nectarine grew, covered in little red spiders, a tree that despite its inhospitable surroundings and the near-constant draught (R.S. would often forget to close the glass doors at night) produced rich and plentiful fruit under Elsi's devoted care.

Separateness was a way of life at Manafon, with R.S. and Elsi's relationship captured in the first line of his poem 'Marriage' (1975): 'I look up; you pass.' Yet theirs was a shared space containing unspoken understanding: 'You have your battle,/too' ('Marriage'). R.S. was a self-confessed loner and his perception of Elsi was that she shared his outlook, mirroring his moods, 'Sighing, if one sighs' ('Anniversary', 1961). They slept in their own rooms, Elsi at the top of the house, R.S. on the second floor in the main bedroom, which had two single beds. Gwydion was 18 before he saw a double bed. His room was reassuringly close to that of his mother and from his window he could see the red squirrels leaping from one alder tree to another along the river bank. The bedrooms were accessed by a web of staircases – front, back and servants' – with a set of rooms above the kitchen that were part of Elsi's domain.

There were no visitors at Manafon. So little happened that when the only child of that silent, withdrawn household once saw someone walking down the long drive he was so astonished that he ran out to find out what could possibly

Elsi transposed the implacable elements of the Welsh terrain into her paintings,
here the landscape around R. S. Thomas's curacy at Chirk.

have caused such a rare event. It was a seclusion that R.S. consciously cultivated: 'I have always sought out lonely places,' he wrote. 'I don't wish to be autocratic because there are those who find association with other human beings both a solace and an enrichment but, mercifully, there has always been an eremitical element in Christianity.'

R.S. took no newspapers, the couple did not entertain, and a television was unimaginable. The silence in the crumbling rectory was profound, interrupted only by the sound of R.S. banging out his own poems on thin paper on his old typewriter. Only those he thought good enough were typed up, the rest were crumpled and cast on the fire later that evening, the detritus of the day's production. R.S. spent the mornings in his ground-floor study reading material that was philosophical in nature or the work of other poets. 'There were weeks when nobody said anything in our house,' Gwydion later commented. Elsi's niece, who occasionally visited, remembered how as a 12-year-old girl she was disturbed by strange noises in the night. She crept downstairs to find her aunt and uncle, he like a great black crow, sitting at a table in silence, reading, a Brahms concert on the wireless. Neither looked up, neither spoke, and she scuttled back to her room, unacknowledged.

Although he admitted to having had one or two friends at Bangor, R.S. no longer kept in touch with them. 'What is a friend, someone you see often? I can't afford to go sixty or seventy miles in a car to say "How do?"' However, there were some local acquaintances, for example Gwendoline and Margaret Davies at Gregynog Hall, three miles away. These sisters were well-known art patrons, amassing one of the great British art collections of the twentieth century that included works by J. M. W. Turner, Claude Monet and Paul Cézanne, as well as establishing a music festival and a private press at their home and hosting visitors such as George Bernard Shaw and Gustav Holst. It was a stimulating household, where even the servants were chosen for their singing voices. Elsi, who painted in an almost bare studio at Manafon, was covetous of Gwen Davies's workroom that had 'shelves around the entire room with racks underneath full of unused canvases'. She was not, however, envious of what was produced in that well-appointed room. 'Gwen painted rather half-hearted landscapes,' was Elsi's cool appraisal.

Every morning Elsi worked in her studio while Gwydion played next door, their separate world filled with the intoxicating smell of turpentine mixed with that of the 'Gloire de Dijon' roses that grew at the back of the house. She drew on her surroundings for inspiration, their own goat appearing in her children's story, *Gwenno the Goat*, published in 1957, and her treasures – assorted dead birds and animal skulls collected from the Manafon garden and hillsides – used for her paintings and illustrations, including those she did for animal stories by Dorothy Richards, such as *Roma Rabbit's Picnic* published by Faber & Faber in 1948. The additional income was a welcome supplement to R.S.'s annual salary of £361.

Gwydion also featured in Elsi's work, most notably in the spectacular allegorical mural *The Dance of Life*, a nearly 30-metre-long commission for the hospital at Gobowen, near Chirk. Too large for the top-floor studio, many of the six panels were painted in the dining room with the door that led to the hall locked up to give the necessary run of canvas. Alongside Gwydion, there are girls, dogs, flowers, birds and animals, all taken from the Manafon landscape. 'I suppose, in all, they contained almost every good idea that I had ever had till then,' she wrote of the panels in her memoirs. Hers was a large, all-encompassing canvas where nature and life merged, and in this monumental work we find an equivalent to R.S.'s poetic vision, as expressed in 'The Village', where parochial detail contains universal truths:

Stay, then, village, for round you spins
On slow axis a world as vast
And meaningful as any posed
By great Plato's solitary mind.

Elsi's epic painting earned the straitened household £900 when it was commissioned in 1951, as well as providing a lasting testament to the talents of Manafon's less-celebrated artistic resident; it is now at Glyndŵr University in Wrexham. R.S.'s one mention of his wife's great painting is in *Autobiographies* (1997), where, commenting briskly on the move in 1954 from Manafon to Eglwys-fach, he observed that his 'poor wife was in the middle of making a mural for the hospital at Gobowen, but she agreed to take her canvas down off the wall in Manafon, and move to the new house'.

The store cupboard of the Manafon gardens provided the raw materials for Elsi's more domestic creations: moleskin purses, berets and rabbit-skin waistcoats, perhaps inspired by memories of the time spent with the fur dealer and his family in Paris. The young Gwydion had no choice but to wear these garments, despite their pungent smell. She also made cushion covers, handkerchiefs and lampshades that she sewed, piercing holes through the pleats with a leather punch.

In addition to her duties inside the house and tending to the rectory garden, Elsi fulfilled her role as rector's wife with humour and grace. Parishioners remember her mucking in socially. Attractive and amusing, she was also practical, on one occasion offering to mend a neighbour's broken windowpane, even cutting the glass herself and bringing the putty to fix it into place. 'I can't imagine him doing that,' was the neighbour's verdict on the rector.

Elsi was also in charge of Manafon Sunday school, and later wrote fondly in her memoirs of the ten small children, each of whom was supposed to learn and repeat a verse from the Bible every Sunday. Only the 'proper' little girls could remember the verse, while the boys would simply repeat the one line that stuck in their minds: 'There cum a leopard and worshipped him.' 'Never having heard of a "leper", this seemed to them a miraculous happening,' Elsi wrote, 'a leopard prostrating itself in a flurry of rippling spots and golden colour. They never forgot it.' R.S. sometimes made an appearance and it was usually memorable: '[He] for some reason asked them what kind of tree was in the Garden of Eden. Tom Belan Deg leapt up, hand raised. "Cooker, sir."'

R.S.'s attitude to children was unreconstructed. His reference to his own son as 'a bit of flesh' is almost cruel in its starkness. He had no small talk thus some of his parochial visits were painful in the extreme. He would sit in the kitchen of his parishioners, neither party wanting to be there, popping bits of bread into his mouth. He often forgot people's names and could be distracted and awkward. When he made a 'social' visit to Philip Larkin in Hull, the latter commented on his visitor in a letter: 'Arsewipe Thomas was led into my room one afternoon last week, and stood there without moving or speaking: he seems pretty hard going. Not noticeably Welsh, which was one comfort.' The epithet alludes to the fact that, according to his biographer Byron Rogers, R.S. was a bit of a snob.

The Revd Canon Donald Allchin later described R.S. as in some ways a 'dead loss' as a parson, but Gwydion demurred, describing him as 'a perfectly competent parish priest'. Allchin did concede that at moments of real crisis R.S. could be 'wonderfully present and helpful', his concern for his parishioners clearly evident. Whereas this obscure parish might have engendered misery in some of his fellow clergy, for R.S., with no desire for preferment, it was ideal: 'Think of taking on Birmingham!' he mused. 'How can you believe you're fit to be spiritual father to three million Brummies?'

As Allchin observed, even if R.S. could be harsh and uncompromising, behind the curmudgeon there was a reserve of kindness. He started a youth club called the Young Wales Club, and one afternoon decided to play a few party games with the members. 'He was all right,' one of the attendees told Byron Rogers, 'he did have ideas. I remember he introduced the game of musical chairs, only of course we didn't have any music. So he used to wink.' As the owner of the only car in the village, he would drive his parishioners on numerous trips to doctors or to visit sick relatives in distant hospitals. He also involved himself in the conventional rounds of parish duties, reporting dutifully in the parish magazine on 'A scrumptious tea in the hall', or a Wolf Cub outing where 'much fun was had'.

When it came to justifying the workings of God to his flock a few party games could be pretty blunt. His explanatory entry in the parish magazine after the death of a 5-year-old child read: 'Thus does God deal with us in ways we cannot understand.' Although he often visited the dying, he felt he could offer no real comfort, only observe; a sense of impotence he captured in his poem 'Evans' (1958) about William Evans, a parishioner well known to the rector who died on 6 February 1946 following an accident:

> It was the dark
> Silting the veins of that sick man
> I left stranded upon the vast
> And lonely shore of his bleak bed.

The local inhabitants were a rich source of material for R.S. There is at times anger and disdain in his attitude towards them: he immortalized Iago Prytherch as 'Just an ordinary man of the bald Welsh hills, ... with a half-witted grin' in 'A Peasant' (1946) – but there is also respect. In Iago he also finds nobility, casting him as 'a winner of wars, / Enduring like a tree under the curious stars.'

But Manafon was not remote enough for the restless R.S. – there was too much garden, not enough Welsh spoken and, although for Elsi and Gwydion it was close enough to Eden, it was time to move further west. A tearful Elsi explained to Gwydion that his father needed more sea and sky. In fact, what he got at Eglwys-fach, on the Dovey estuary on the coast of mid-Wales, was a prim

Illustration from *Gwenno the Goat*, 1957, by M. E. Eldridge.

R. S. Thomas in 1964, photographed by Jane Bown.

small vicarage with a tidy garden and rounds of tea and cocktail parties with retired army officers, and unwelcome gentility. 'The smell of the farmyard was replaced by the smell of the decayed conscience,' he wrote in *The Echoes Return Slow* (1988). His journey did not stop until he reached Aberdaron, a village at the furthest tip of the Llŷn peninsula where the Thomases lived from 1967 to 1978. This is a parish so far west that the sea sweeps against the edges of the churchyard and the vicarage stands big and bleak, an ecclesiastical last stand before the vast greyness of the Irish Sea. Here R.S. took his place in a line of vicars reaching back to 1291, finally 'made free/by the tide's pendulum truth', as he wrote in 'At the End' (1995).

By the time R.S. arrived at Aberdaron he was already an established literary figure with a reputation that had won him the Queen's Medal for Poetry in 1964. His standing was further enhanced by the poetry collections *Laboratories of the Spirit* (1975) and *Frequencies* (1978), the latter published the same year that he and Elsi retired to Sarn-y-Plas at Rhiw, also on the Llŷn peninsula. Here, he continued to produce poetry and, 'driven to think' on the edge of Wales, he became a forceful figure for Welsh nationalism. By now a fluent Welsh speaker, his voice reclaimed for the Welsh nation its culture, language and heritage. It was a vision he asserted loudly and publicly and not without controversy, vociferously supporting the Welsh nationalist movement Meibion Glyndŵr's policy of setting fire to English holiday homes in the principality as well as endorsing the Campaign for Nuclear Disarmament. Nominated for the Nobel Prize for Literature in 1996, he died four years later aged 87, a fiercely independent Welsh cleric acclaimed as one of the finest twentieth-century poets in the English language.

Looking back in the poem 'Manafon' (included in *Residues*, published posthumously in 2002), there was a wistful, late acknowledgment of all that the balanced, handsome rectory had embodied, for him as well as for Elsi and Gwydion:

> What
> it was saying to the unasked
> question was: 'The answer
> is here.'

CHAPTER SEVEN

Rooms of Verse

George Herbert and Vikram Seth at Bemerton

O N A RAINY SUNDAY IN JUNE 2003, the Indian novelist and poet Vikram Seth (b. 1952) drove to the small parish of Bemerton on the outskirts of Salisbury in Wiltshire to view a rectory that had recently come on the market. It had been the home of George Herbert (1593–1633) and the name of one his favourite poets had jumped out at Seth when he had been glancing through a friend's newspaper, as he recorded in his own poem 'Host' (2011): 'I heard it was for sale and thought I'd go/To see the old house where/He lived three years, and died.' A self-declared urban dweller, Seth, who had won international acclaim for his novel *A Suitable Boy* in 1993, nonetheless found himself drawn to the building where George Herbert had lived as rector.

At first sight, the rectory is modestly handsome but unremarkable. It sits right on the lower road that runs through the parish, almost within touching distance of the tiny church of St Andrew's that stands opposite. Part of the north side abutting the road dates from 1470 and includes a three-storey gabled block of chequered flint and stone. Herbert made changes to the building when he beame the rector in 1630, and although there have been additions over the centuries, reflecting the varying needs of a long line of incumbents, at its core Bemerton Rectory remains a powerful projection of Herbert's vision. He lived there for just three years, yet he left an indelible impression not only on the rectory itself, not least in the instruction to his successors carved in stone on the building's façade, but also on the church, the parish and, through his poetry, on English literary culture.

St Andrew's Church and the Old Rectory at Bemerton. Herbert's poetic legacy to his successors, in a stone plaque above the door of the rectory, is still visible from the road, reminding them to 'Be good to the poor'.

Within these walls Herbert worked on his 'Mark to aim at', the precepts for the parish priest: *A Priest to the Temple* (also known as *The Country Parson His Character and Rule of Holy Life*; 1652). In this guide he showed how to structure and shape the response of the human to the divine. The parson's home, in Herbert's vision, became the channel for such communion, order and godliness. He understood the central position the rectory held in society and how its moral architecture, replicated throughout the land, could be a force for good. He did not live to see his dream realized; indeed, within a decade of his death the stand-off between Charles I and Parliament had developed into full-scale civil war. In his poem 'Church Militant', however, Herbert showed that he appreciated how conflict would propel religion westward: 'Religion stands on tiptoe in our land/Readie to pass to the *American* strand.' At its heart, Herbert's work exemplifies the struggle between the public and the private, the human and the divine. At Bemerton, he could work through the paradox and doubt that formed an intrinsic part of his faith.

These spiritual struggles formed part of Herbert's attraction for Seth. He first came across Herbert's poetry as an 8-year-old growing up in India; he took his mother's copy of *The Albatross Book of Verse* to boarding school in Dehradun where, as he recalled later, he 'dipped into it from time to time', enjoying the poet's wordplay. A few years after this, at Tonbridge School in England, Seth was assigned a collection of Herbert's verse, edited by R. S. Thomas, as a set text for A-level and he found he had an affinity with Herbert and 'his clarity, his depth of feeling, his spiritual struggles ... his delight in the pleasures of nature and music, his wit'. Although Seth describes himself as neither Christian nor particularly religious, Herbert is still one of his favourite poets; it was sufficient to inspire him to drive down a motorway on a grey and wet day to see the place where so many of Herbert's best-loved poems had been written.

Seth had no real intention of buying the house, but once he saw what he refers to in 'Host' as Herbert's 'rooms of verse' and experienced its atmosphere he was tempted to make an offer. He walked across the lane into the church and in a stained-glass window he saw an image of Herbert holding, somewhat surprisingly, a violin. 'My partner at that time was Philippe Honoré, the violinist,' Seth recalled. 'I took this as a happy sign.' His mind made up, Seth became custodian of Herbert's rectory, taking up his literary legacy and securing his secular place in Bemerton's rich history.

At first the spirit of Herbert and the poetry of the past haunted Seth's imagination. 'I felt his presence hourly,' he remembers. It was not hard to conjure an image of the poet-rector writing in his room, looking towards the church in quiet contemplation; or walking down through the garden, across the river Nadder that runs through the grounds, and over the water meadows to Salisbury Cathedral for Evensong. Seth admits that if the house had belonged to Milton or some other more forceful personality he would not have been able to live there: 'But Herbert, for all his depth and richness, is a clear writer and a quiet spirit. He might influence me but would not wish to wrest me from myself.'

As time passed, Seth felt less of a guest in his own home, happy to acknowledge the shared poetic space, writing in 'Host': 'Though far in time and faith, I share his tears, / His hearth, his ground, his mud'. Seth explains that he 'was inhabiting Herbert's stanzas in both senses of the word'. Although distance in terms of 'time and faith' is recognized, Seth feels and states a profound connection with his tactful host. This is literally the case, too, as the large rectory hearth is still *in situ* in the kitchen; and when the river Nadder overflows its banks and floods the rectory gardens, the receding waters leave a muddy residue just as they did during Herbert's brief tenure.

For George Herbert, Bemerton was the culmination of a circuitous journey that began on 3 April 1593 at Black Hall in Montgomeryshire, where he was born into a 'Generous, *Noble*, and Ancient Family', according to Barnabas Oley, author of the preface to *Herbert's Remains* (1652), a collection of Herbert's works published after his death. He was the fourth son in this family of ten children, and whereas his brothers achieved worldly success in politics, at court and in the army and navy, he was to find greater and enduring fame (although with a far smaller audience during his lifetime as his poems written in English were all published posthumously) from a humble parish rectory.

Herbert was only 3 when his father died, and the formative influence in his life then became his mother, the remarkable Magdalen Newport. This formidable matriarch knew how important education and patronage would be for her offspring, so she moved them to the sophisticated spheres of Oxford where they would have access to the best tutors. Two years later, in 1601, the family moved to London where she held a busy, sociable salon in her house, first in Charing Cross and then in Chelsea. A friend to John Donne – she was the subject of his sonnet 'The Autumnal', and after her death he delivered a

The seventeenth-century friends and scholars Nicholas Ferrar and George Herbert are depicted in a stained-glass window in St Andrew's Church, Bemerton. Ferrar was Herbert's literary executor.

commemorative address about her – Magdalen had a profound influence on Herbert. Physically striking, she understood the importance of image and matched it with an inner quest for moral perfection. She combined beauty with enough drive and energy to mobilize a family of ten while also managing to attract a younger second husband who was so handsome that people ran after him in the street to express their admiration. Hers was a godly, disciplined and ordered household, following the domestic rules laid out in an entry in her *Kitchen Booke* dated 11 April 1603, the year another independent and powerful woman, Elizabeth I, died and passed the throne to James VI of Scotland who became James I of England.

Successfully tutored at home and Westminster School, where he was already composing Latin verse, the young Herbert went up to Trinity College, Cambridge, in 1609, a brilliant scholar but perhaps a little too conscious of his 'parts and parentage' according to Izaak Walton, his first biographer. He was soon noticed by the King, who had an eye for good-looking men and dubbed Herbert 'the jewel of that University'. With such admirers, it is not surprising that following his graduation in 1613 he became a Fellow of Trinity and by 1620 had risen to be Public Orator at Cambridge. This post brought him into contact with the highest in the land since it involved the composition and delivery of letters and speeches to the King himself, as well as visiting dignitaries. It also gave the talented Herbert a public platform from which to launch a career at court if he so wished. The court of James I was a dissipated, if glamorous place to be, but a curious world to inhabit for the man who would be remembered as the 'saintly Mr Herbert'. At the time, however, he was short of money, as frustrated letters to his stepfather reveal, and kingly and aristocratic patronage was difficult to refuse. There would always be tension between the worldly and the spiritual aspects of his life, but at this point the secular held sway. Among his other positions, Herbert was elected MP for Montgomery, a family tradition, in 1624 and was ordained deacon in the same year.

When James I died in 1625, Herbert's worldly ambition seems to have died with him. The loss compounded that of the death the previous year of another of his patrons, the Duke of Lennox. Herbert himself had never enjoyed good health and following the devastating loss of his mother in 1627 he became very ill, possibly with the turberculosis that would claim him six years later. At this point, however, he recovered enough to turn away from what Izaak Walton reported as 'the painted pleasures' of court life and took Holy Orders.

In 1629, the ancient but modest living of Bemerton bordering the estate at Wilton where his aristocratic relations lived, was offered to Herbert by Charles I, 'if it be worth his acceptance', in response to petitions from the family. The newly married Herbert was hesitant about accepting a lowly posting in a village of only three hundred souls – 'yet my soul drew back' – but on 26 April 1630 he was instituted Rector of Bemerton by Bishop Davenant, his induction taking place in the former chapel of ease of St Andrew's. Nearly four hundred years later, Vikram Seth would follow Herbert's footsteps and have his tenure at Bemerton confirmed in the same church – although in his case, by the 'sign' of Herbert clutching a violin, rather than Herbert's dramatic prostration in front of the altar.

Both men faced a rebuild, although Herbert's was rather more radical because the rectory had lain empty for a decade. Since the Reformation, rectories had evolved considerably, been altered, had decayed or even been demolished, all reflections of the changing needs, income and status of the incumbent (who, after the break with Rome, could now marry and have a family), with his multiple roles in the parish as well as his position in charge of the cure of souls. The upkeep of the rectory was a challenge for most rectors. Church livings, where the income was directly related to the profitability of farming and therefore tithes, were not held at a constant level and changed with economic circumstance. When agricultural productivity fell away, reduced circumstances would often turn a parish priest's thoughts to personal rather than heavenly requirements, and the maintenance of the fabric of the rectory and the church suffered accordingly.

For Herbert, rebuilding was both a moral duty and a practical necessity. He recognized that historically society's structures, social and religious, were utilized to keep dislocation and disorder at bay. When he arrived at Bemerton, the country was troubled. Parliament had been disbanded in 1629, there were rumblings against the King from anti-Catholics as well as Puritans, and the Church of England, politically aligned with the Crown, was in disarray, a further reason for the state of disrepair of its properties. Against this shifting and con-fusing backdrop, William Laud (Archbishop of Canterbury, 1633–45) would attempt to impose order from the top down. Herbert who, like the ambitious Laud, linked order to godliness, also sought to shore up the nation's spiritual life, but from the bottom up, through the visible instruments of his church and rectory.

A drawing of George Herbert on vellum by Robert White, thought to be the
original drawing from which all subsequent likenesses were taken.

The first task was to rebuild St Andrew's. In this, Herbert followed his own advice given in *A Priest to the Temple*: 'The Country Parson hath a speciall care of his Church, that all things there be decent, and befitting his Name by which it is called. Therefore first he takes order, that all things be in good repair; as walls plaistered, windows glazed, floore paved, seats whole, firm, and uniform ... Secondly that the Church be swept, and kept cleane without dust, or Cobwebs, and at great festivalls strawed, and stuck with boughs, and perfumed with incense.'

Herbert had started his programme of church rebuilding in 1626 at Leighton Bromswold, near Huntingdon, after he was appointed deacon, refitting the church at his own expense, much to the dismay of his mother who protested: 'George, it is not for your weak body, and empty purse to undertake to build churches.' Nicholas Ferrar, Herbert's friend and Cambridge contemporary, strove for similar perfection in the church architecture at the community his family established in Little Gidding, only five miles from Leighton Bromswold. In this remote, decaying parish Ferrar transformed the pigsty-barn of the abandoned church into a model of simplicity and worship. It became a place of pilgrimage even during his lifetime, and was later honoured by T. S. Eliot who named one of his *Four Quartets* 'Little Gidding', commemorating a place 'where prayer has been valid'. It was to Ferrar that Herbert's papers were sent after his death, giving him instructions to publish any of the material he thought worthy, but to destroy the bundle of manuscripts if not.

In Herbert's view, the church was the first instrument pointing the way to divine apprehension. He believed that through reading the simple messages built into the actual framework of the church all who worshipped there would be brought to a state of individual godliness. In his poem 'The Church-floore', Herbert guides the reader at a very intimate level around his church: 'Mark you the floore? that square & speckled stone, / Which looks so firm and strong, / Is *Patience*'. Thus he proceeds, pointing out the black and white 'checker'd' arrangement of 'Humilitie' on another area of the church's floor, the 'Confidence' of the 'Quire' (choir), even the 'sweet cement' binding 'Love / And Charitie'. All this, when collected and presented as a complete map of the church layout, allows the onlooker to find his own way to the divine. Architectural signs, thus assimilated, opened a route to profound spiritual truths. Other visual elements were similarly texts to be read. A stained-glass window, for example, was a filter through which to approach heaven:

A man that looks on glasse,
On it may stay his eye;
Or if he pleaseth, through it passe,
And then the heav'n espie.

Once the church at Bemerton had been reconstructed, Herbert turned his attention to the rectory. The building should be a text for men to decipher godliness, yet it must also be a home to the private man in his domestic and 'fallen' state, that humble parson who was also, paradoxically, 'the priest to the temple', the mouthpiece and interpreter of the divine.

The 1616 terrier or land register of Bemerton describes the rectory as a modest glebe, and by the time Herbert arrived it was 'fall'n down or decayd', neglected by his predecessor, Walter Curle, who had chosen to live at the much finer parsonage house of his other parish of Mildenhall, over twenty miles away. The rectory needed to be three parts rebuilt, and Herbert could ill afford it. He wrote to his brother that the works had made him 'beggarly': he had already spent the large sum of £200 and had seen 'nothing yett' in terms of tithe returns.

Herbert's restoration is traceable, despite extensive additions and changes to the structure in the eighteenth and nineteenth centuries. The central part of the house had been modelled in the late fifteenth century on the lines of an English hall, and in 1630 it still had one large central room downstairs where most domestic activities took place. Stores and a tithe barn once stood to the west of the hall. The staircase leads to the bedrooms and the room where Herbert died. The poet and his wife, Jane Danvers, a relative of Herbert's step-father, were childless, but they provided a home for Jane's two nieces from the time they moved to Bemerton.

There are two aspects to the rectory: the public façade visible to the parish and the private one, indicative of the devotional life, hidden from general view. Looking back from the river, the rectory offers a very different sight from the restrained flint and stone exterior on the road. From here, the building presents its magical side, a mellow frontage standing serenely in its own fine English gardens, the lawns running gently down to the river with the water meadows of Salisbury beyond. The two distinct vistas from Herbert's bedroom encompass this dual aspect; from one window can be seen the grand spire of Salisbury Cathedral, the imposing reality of the power of the Established Church, while

The Old Rectory at Bemerton, viewed from the garden.

viewed from the other, almost within touching distance, is St Andrew's, testament to the more intimate nature of his worship and ministry.

For Herbert, internal holiness was declared through personal appearance. This view was translated to the fabric of the rectory itself, which must avoid all luxury, 'a very visible sinne'. 'Neatnesse', on the other hand, declared ordered spirituality, and cleanliness was next to godliness. Monastic rigour – chastity – was Herbert's preferred state for a country parson ('virginity is a higher state than matrimony'), though if a parson was to marry then his wife should be chosen according to her fitness for parochial duties rather than by 'the eye' of 'his affection'. Fortunately, Jane seems to have fitted both criteria, described by her relation John Aubrey in *Brief Lives* as 'a handsome bona roba and ingeniose'.

Self-discipline was all important. The country parson should not only be strict in the governing of his house, but also 'exceeding exact in his Life, being holy, just, prudent, temperate, bold, grave in all his wayes'. This was clearly no longer normal conduct because, according to Herbert, the average country parson in 1630 had become a figure of contempt, far from his ideal: 'he must be an absolute Master and commander of himself.' Drunkenness was to be avoided; as the most popular vice aligned 'with the unfruitfull works of darknesse', it drew Herbert's particular censure.

Herbert dealt in ideals, but he recognized that his parishioners were bound to fall far below his mark, country people being 'full of these petty injustices, being cunning to make use of another, and spare themselves'. (In this disparaging view, Herbert was later to find a worthy successor in R. S. Thomas.) It was their parson's duty to offer them practical as well as spiritual support and he would achieve this through a very public ministry, maintaining a visible presence among his flock, not just by performing his duties within the church but by going out into the fields to see his parishioners, 'wallowing in the midst of their affairs', to settle differences and bless the fruits of their labour. It was the rector's duty to overcome the stench of some of the cottages (which Herbert describes in almost bestial language), however unpleasant the task, especially for one used to the fragrant and painted pleasures of court: 'though he even creep into it, and though it smell never so lothsomely. For both God is there also.'

The rectory was the purifying force. Restraint governed its furnishings. In his description of the parson's ideal home, Herbert prescribed furniture that 'is very plain, but clean, whole, and sweet, as sweet as his garden can make; for he hath no mony for such things, charity being his only perfume'. Around the family table at Bemerton the walls were 'not idle, but something is written, or painted there, which may excite the reader to a thought of piety; especially the 101 Psalm, which is expressed in a fayre table, as being the rule of a family'. Such decorative memento mori were designed to shore up Christian fortitude against 'the cold midnight storms of persecution and adversity'. They may also have acted as part of Herbert's armory against 'the proper and peculiar temptations of [the parson's] state of life' that required constant vigilance.

Herbert's mind was rarely settled and his spiritual quest, with which Seth feels such affinity, continued even in the comparatively resolved atmosphere of Bemerton. The need for such structure was there, too, in his poetry. The layout of poems such as 'Easter Wings' or 'The Altar', for example, which are arranged on the page to illustrate their subject matter, echoes his attempt to shape the relevance of faith in this world. Such literary architecture is appropriated by Vikram Seth in the form of his poem 'Oak' (2011), which is laid out in an hourglass pattern in Alec Roth's notation of its musical setting, mirroring the oak tree in Bemerton's water meadow, its leafless branches reflected in the pooled water below. For Seth the homage is part of his ongoing dialogue with Herbert, not one based on a shared faith perhaps, but in the exploration of mysticism rooted in nature and humanity, mapped out in the text of his collection of libretti and prose *The Rivered Earth* (2011).

Alongside prayer and teaching, cleanliness, wholesome food, decent manners and self-sufficiency were Herbert's prescription for domestic life in the country rectory: 'His fare is plain, and common, but wholsome, what hee hath, is little, but very good; it consisteth most of mutton, beefe and veal, if he addes any thing for a great day, or a stranger, his garden or orchard supplyes it, or his barne.' Herbert clearly lived by his own precepts as he was 'lean to an extremity'. Like many rural rectors since, he knew the importance of diet and its effect on the health of his parishioners. Bad digestion was a particular obsession: 'And obstructions are the cause of most diseases,' he wrote with authority.

Such 'obstructions' could be remedied by the herbs and plants grown in the rectory garden. Herbert recommended the sixteenth-century French medical practitioner Fernelius as the best source for physic and advised the parson, who should 'be all to his Parish, and not onely a Pastour, but a Lawyer also, and a Phisician', to 'make the garden the shop: For home-bred medecines

¶ Eafter wings.

Lord, who createdft man in wealth and ftore,
Though foolifhly he loft the fame,
Decaying more and more,
Till he became
Moft poore:
With thee
O let me rife
As larks, harmonioufly,
And fing this day thy victories:
Then fhall the fall further the flight in me.

Eafter

¶ Eafter wings.

My tender age in forrow did beginne
And ftill with fickneffes and fhame
That I became
Moft thinne.
With thee
Let me combine,
And feel this day thy victorie:
For, if I imp my wing on thine,
Affliction fhall advance the flight in me.

H. Ba-

'Easter Wings', an example of George Herbert's pattern poetry.

George Herbert at Bemerton, 1860, by William Dyce. The poet-rector's lute can be seen resting against the stone bench and his fishing rod and basket leaning on the tree by the river Nadder. The spire of Salisbury Cathedral is visible in the background.

are both more easie for the Parsons purse, and more familiar for all mens bodyes.' Sickness and disease were a constant threat. Plague had provoked an exodus from Salisbury in 1627, and would return again in 1636. Despite the dangers of contagion, Herbert decreed that the rectory door must be 'ever-open'. From his arrival at Bemerton, mortality was a constant presence, with 'Death, working like a mole' inside him, as Walton wrote. Herbert's tuberculosis lay dormant, but perhaps exacerbated by the damp atmosphere rising from his beloved river Nadder it would claim his life three years later.

Herbert found inspiration in the garden, creating in poems such as 'The Flower' a lyrical framework with which to approach the divine. The garden is also the setting for the famous painting of Herbert by William Dyce, an imaginary evocation of the poet-rector walking beside the Nadder, with his lute resting against a stone bench (Aubrey said he had 'a very good hand on the lute') and a fishing rod and basket leaning against a tree, created in 1860 when Dyce was the guest of the then rector, T. H. Wyatt. The spire of Salisbury Cathedral can be glimpsed in the distance, the source of Herbert's 'heaven upon earth' where he could enjoy liturgical music, adding his voice to the choir at Evensong, followed by a private musical meeting. Music always had the power to revive his 'drooping spirits' and until the morning of his death, a month before his fortieth birthday, he greeted the day in waking song, even, according to Walton, rising from his deathbed to sing verses from his poems 'Sunday' and 'The Thanksgiving.' He was buried in the church opposite in an unmarked grave near the altar, ensuring that, despite the brevity of his tenure, his name will always be associated with the parish.

Herbertian harmonies persist and have been taken up and reworked by Seth, responding to his host's poetic voice, which is discernible, but not over-whelming. Since he has been 'inhabiting his rooms and stanzas', Seth has written six poems modelled on Herbert's verse forms. The fourth of these, 'Host', echoes the form, structure and sentiment of Herbert's 'Love III': 'Love bade me welcome …' It is a self-conscious dialogue with his poetic forebear and an acknowledgment of his kindly influence.

The river Nadder is also a constant presence for Herbert's successor. In 'Confluences', a collaborative project conceived and written at Bemerton by Seth and the composer Alec Roth, Seth's poems are set to Roth's music, continuing Herbert's harmonious melding of poetry and music. This work was developed around the kitchen table and at the large black piano in the rectory's

The view of Salisbury Cathedral has barely changed since the period when George Herbert walked through the water meadows from Bemerton on his way to Evensong.

red room overlooking the garden. The notion that informs the work is directly linked to the river, where the flow of ideas, geographies and cultures merge and meld into a cohesive whole just as diverse tributaries flow into the ancient watercourse. The Nadder is thus transposed into one small part of the universal pattern of waterways covering and connecting the planet.

Seth and Roth took the same path as Herbert when they were looking for inspiration. They found it in the unchanging landscape, in the leafless branches of the oak tree reflected in the water, like roots reaching down into the depths of the river itself. Such walks across the water meadows also revealed secret bridges, connections in the landscape that became Roth's 'ponticellis', linking the separate librettis of the work of 'Shared Ground' to form a coherent entity. Not just an interior landscape for composition, the water meadows show another side to Bemerton as a place of moods and mystery, revealing itself only partially, as in the brief glimpse Roth had of one of the bridges discovered in his wanderings, a 'Bridge of Sighs' that, inexplicably, once seen he could never find again.

At Bemerton Herbert found a sense of what Seth recognizes as 'hard-earned stillness'. In this spirit he was able to dedicate his life to the care of his parishioners and, in the rectory itself, discovered the place where 'I might sing,/And serve thee;' ('The Crosse'). His poetic legacy established him as one of the greatest metaphysical and devotional poets in the language and the first edition of *The Temple: Sacred Poems and Private Ejaculations*, edited by Nicholas Ferrar and published in 1633, had run through six editions by 1641. Charles I is reputed to have had a copy with him in his cell at Carisbrooke Castle prior to his execution in London in 1649. Herbert's admirers range from other seventeenth-century poets, such as Richard Crashaw and Henry Vaughan, through to T. S. Eliot, R. S. Thomas and Seamus Heaney in our own time. From a small parish in Wiltshire Herbert's reputation spread as far as America, where his style is discernible in the work of the early poets Edward Taylor and Philip Pain.

Herbert's consoling voice can still be heard by Seth in the rectory at Bemerton where he 'directly tempers' the novelist's turmoil. In 'Host', Seth acknowledges the poet-rector's quiet presence and tacit sympathy:

Yet my host stands just out of mind and sight,
That I may sit and write.

CHAPTER EIGHT

This Entertainment
is Inexhaustible

The Benson and de Waal families at Lincoln

B EYOND PARISH BOUNDARIES, the clerical buildings of the cathedral close
have proved to be equally rich breeding grounds for literary voices.
The Chancery at Lincoln is one such place. A large, rambling house of
medieval origin, mystery and intrigue are built into its very fabric. There are
cavernous vaulted cellars, winding stone staircases, endless passageways, and
ancient plumbing systems making unexplained noises in twilit attic rooms.

The Chancery stands opposite the east window of the great Gothic
cathedral of Lincoln, an architectural spectacle that has dominated the city for
some eight hundred years. In the early 1970s, the young Edmund de Waal grew
up exploring its vast interior (and later that of the cathedral at Canterbury). The
shadow cast by those medieval cathedrals had a profound influence on de Waal's
work as a ceramic artist; their giant scale echoed in the locations of some of his
installations. 'I think part of my early experiences of wandering through buildings and feeling different kinds of spaces was very, very important,' de Waal
confirms. 'I do remember being startled by how beautiful and interesting and
odd a lot of the spaces in those cathedrals were.' In the rhythms and counter-
rhythms of the pointed arches and choir vaulting, other, unknown lives are
hinted at. Voices of the past are linked to the present in this place where worship
has been conducted for centuries. Here the invisible is made visible, the tension
of opposites made architectural reality.

This huge brooding church, rising majestically above the Fenland mists, is
perhaps underappreciated and underloved by the nation at large. But it was

174

cherished by that most famous of neo-Gothic architects, A. W. N. Pugin, who drew much inspiration from it. He returned to Lincoln to add his own architectural element to the evolving story of the close in the form of the bede or prayer houses (rent to be paid by bede or prayer.) These small symmetrical houses set around a cloister garden embody Pugin's vision of Christian values in architecture and remain in use today.

The cathedral has cast its spell on religious and secular visitors alike. In his novel *The Rainbow* (1915), D. H. Lawrence, not a church-goer, nonetheless described the powerful sense of wonder and awe evoked by Lincoln Cathedral. In the building's columned gloom Anna Brangwen senses 'the very essence of life'. This 'coloured darkness ... whereof life's day would blossom and fall away again, re-echoed peace and profound immemorial silence ... Here, in the church, "before" and "after" were folded together, all was contained in oneness.'

To the de Waal children, the joy of living in the Chancery was not confined to its proximity to the ineffable presence of the cathedral, but extended to exploring the eccentric fabric of the house itself. In this they had been preceded, a century before, by the prolifically creative Benson children, who grew up to become the novelist E. F. (Fred) Benson, famous for the *Mapp and Lucia* novels; the poet and later Master of Magdalene College, Cambridge, A. C. (Arthur) Benson, author of the lyrics to that anthem of national pride 'Land of Hope and Glory'; Mary Eleanor (Nellie), writer and essayist on social ills; Margaret (Maggie), a published authority on Egypt, theology and women's education; and Robert Hugh, a writer who went on to become a Catholic priest. The Benson children described the Chancery as a magical place. It was, according to Arthur in his memoir *The Trefoil* (1923),

> a house that might seem to have been designed and constructed solely
> for the delight and satisfaction of children, all mysterious, tortuous,
> inexplicable, with unaccountable spaces and solitudes everywhere.

Inside and out, the Chancery is an engaging, haphazard narrative of the changing architectural tastes and needs of successive chancellors across eight centuries. The brick façade on the street is mostly early Tudor with a stone oriel window fronting the Great Chamber or drawing room, but to the rear there are substantial remains of the buildings erected in the time of Chancellor Antony Bek (1321–29), the most tyrannical of clerics and later a quarrelsome Bishop of

An aerial view of Lincoln. The Chancery, hidden behind the medieval cathedral in this photograph, forms part of the complex of buildings that has grown up around the imposing edifice over the centuries.

Norwich. A medieval solar with a later brick front abuts a three-bay loggia, a somewhat domestic addition built in the mid-twentieth-century by a family-conscious Chancellor to provide a sheltered spot in the garden.

The Chancery has royal connections, too. From 1381 to 1397 it housed the beauteous Katherine Swynford who, although not of noble birth, managed to rise through the ranks of medieval society to become the mistress of John of Gaunt, Duke of Lancaster, and son of Edward III. Described by chroniclers of the time as an 'enchantress', to explain such a meteoric rise in status, she married John in Lincoln Cathedral in 1396 and their descendant was Henry VII, founder of the Tudor dynasty. Her brother-in-law Geoffrey Chaucer, married to her elder sister Philippa, was probably a frequent visitor to the Chancery and worshipper at the cathedral. Philippa was admitted to the Confraternity of Lincoln in 1386, ensuring her name was included in the cathedral prayers and intercessions for her protection in this world and the next.

The romantic legend surrounding the Chancery is counterbalanced by a more malevolent history. The building still bears the scars of its violent past. Cromwell's bullets are lodged in the great wooden doors, testament to a bloody confrontation during the Civil War. There is internal scarring, too, secret signs and symbols carved on the steps of the stone staircase that opens from a nail-studded door in the hall, protective devices left there by medieval stonemasons fearful of satanic intruders.

Chancellors at Lincoln are appointed by the bishop of the day and in the early 1870s Bishop Wordsworth, nephew of the poet, needed an educationalist to establish Lincoln's first theological college. He chose Edward White Benson (1829–96), a driven man who would rise to be Archbishop of Canterbury. Benson had spent nearly fifteen years as the first Master of Wellington College, founded to honour the eponymous duke by educating the 'sons of heroes', though the boys were of a character too coarse for Benson's taste. For the six Benson offspring the ivy-covered Chancery at Lincoln presented a welcome contrast to the dramatic Victorian toughness of Wellington College. Their home at the school had been the impressive Master's Lodge, built in the Gothic style to Edward's own design with tall chimneys, gables, a separate entrance to the Master's study and a drawing room grand enough to entertain royal visitors. Its commanding architecture spoke of a man asserting his will: on the building, on the school and its pupils and, within its walls, on his young wife, Mary, known as Minnie, twelve years his junior.

They had first met when Minnie was 5 and when she was just 12 Benson resolved to marry her. Young and, he thought, malleable, Minnie offered a form of refuge and pliable companionship for Benson. She would later recognize his influence, describing him to a friend as 'the self of myself', although in her retrospective diary she mused that since she did not really love him, she wondered that she 'didn't go more wrong'. Her husband had from an early age struggled with severe depression. His father, a chemical engineer whose business had failed, had died when Benson was 14, leaving the family financially distressed, and as the eldest of the eight children Benson became the patriarch. A strong authoritarian streak, intense self-discipline informed by a taste for theology rooted in liturgy and ritual that would serve him well in his future career in education and the Church, made him a difficult partner and father.

Minnie, however, proved not to be as malleable a wife as he had anticipated and she resisted the authority he had imposed so successfully on Wellington and on the architectural features of the Master's Lodge. Minnie's brother was Henry Sigdwick, the Cambridge agnostic philosopher, and Minnie herself was described by William Gladstone as the cleverest woman in Europe. She was also conflicted both in terms of her faith and her feelings for other women, and after her husband's death in 1896 she would end her days living with Lucy Tait, daughter of Campbell Tait, a former Archbishop of Canterbury.

At Wellington the conflicts were still contained within the structure of the conventional domesticity that Benson had created at the Master's Lodge, although signs of unhappiness were perhaps already perceptible in the gloomy decoration. Arthur, in *The Trefoil*, described the layout as 'well-proportioned ... but all the wood used was pitchpine, and the walls smeared with a chilly-looking, lilac-coloured distemper, on which every hot finger-print of climbing children was visible.' It was not an uplifting environment for the depressive Benson, nor for Minnie.

Against this background the offer in 1872 from Bishop Wordsworth to move to Lincoln as Chancellor was welcome, even if it did involve a drastic reduction in salary for Benson. He was worn down by the role of headmaster and relished the chance to pursue his true calling in the Church in 'the cloistered existence I have always wished for', although it would mean living in 'holy poverty'. Nonetheless, in September 1873, the calm of the cloister was a long way off. Benson was immersed in domestic industry, supervising a team of workmen at the Chancery whose ineptitude became the subject for lighthearted

Edward White Benson, Chancellor of Lincoln, photographed in 1876.
His calm appearance belied a depressive and controlling personality.

The Chancery, Lincoln. The studded panelled double doors (*c.* 1500) to the arched doorway still bear the bullet marks of Cromwell's soldiers.

comment – surprisingly for such a strict and humourless taskmaster – in a letter from the chancellor-foreman to his wife. 'All going well,' he wrote:

> Arrangements are very complete at the Chancery; there is a man to make dust, and a man to burn paint off doors, and a man to make a noise with a hammer, and a man to throw soot at the books, and a man to dig for tobacco pipes in the garden, and a man to splash the paper with paint, and a man to scrape paint off with a knife, and a boy not to fetch or carry, and rods and rings not to fit, and carpets not to fit also, and women to wet floors, and several men to charge.

Eventually the house submitted to Benson's authority. The children went there in an 'ecstasy of delight … and spent the days deliciously in moving furniture and hanging pictures under his direction'. The large sideboard had been brought from the Wellington dining room, along with Minnie's sofa and ottoman. Benson appears to have been obsessed with domestic decoration down to the last detail; at Wellington he had once stormed into the room where Minnie was carrying out secretarial duties on his behalf, 'and made some *very strong* remarks on the subject of the Antimacassars'. It was an area on which they could not agree, Minnie unable to bring herself to engage with matters that she viewed as tedious and unimportant, while for her husband these were issues of moral purpose and as such did not allow for compromise. But the imposition of his will brought some advantages. Volumes of Tennyson, Sir Walter Scott and other literary works adorned the bookshelves in Minnie's private sitting room, arranged and decorated in her absence by her husband with a 'touching care for its brightness'. It was half-panelled, painted white, with a sprigged wallpaper and an orange carpet. 'My father certainly laid the impress of his beautiful taste very firmly on that incredibly picturesque house,' Arthur wrote.

Minnie's comfortable sitting room was enhanced for the children by their mother's presence. She brought light and sun to the room, ensuring that the children always gravitated towards it, sure of a welcome, whatever had happened. Here, every evening, Minnie would read to them from Dickens's novels in front of the fire; in his memoir, *Our Family Affairs* (1920), Fred recalled standing behind her chair 'passing my fingers over the smooth brown hair above her forehead, and listening to the story of the Kenwigses. Her voice and the contact of my fingers on her hair wakened in me the knowledge of how I loved her.'

Minnie Benson (left) with Nellie and Maggie; Beth, the nurse (right), holds Fred, 1869.

Left: Nellie, aged 13, and Maggie, aged 11; Right: Fred, aged 9, and Hugh, aged 5. Lincoln, 1876.

.

Benson's own study was at the centre of the house, below the nursery and above the drawing room. For Arthur, in his stories of childhood, it was a dark place, guarded by two tiger-skin rugs complete with alarmingly lifelike heads. Each night the small boy would have to pass these fearful sentries to bid his father goodnight. He begged the faithful nurse Beth to remain on guard until he had passed safely through to the staircase on the other side of the passage. One night his father emerged from the study and told Beth such watchfulness was over indulgent and unnecessary. The terrified child was mollified only when his mother reinterpreted the tigers as the children's loyal protectors rather than their enemies.

A more peaceful atmosphere was to be found in the oratory, another example of Benson impressing his personality on the design of the house's interior. Until the arrival of his predecessor, Chancellor Massingberd, the ritual of domestic prayers had not always been incorporated into life within the Chancery. Chancellor Pretyman, for example, who died in 1859, had concentrated his efforts on improving the property for his household by adding a vast array of stables, lofts, a granary and coach house at the back of the already sprawling house – all testifying to his wealth and status (guests were attended to in the Chancery dining room by individual footmen stationed behind each chair). Another more sporting inhabitant rarely let his clerical duties interfere with his real interests and was regularly seen dashing straight from morning service – discarding his surplice on the way – to leap into his post-chaise and charge off to Lincoln races.

Benson was to reposition the ritual of prayer at the heart of the Chancery. As a young man, he had created his own secret oratory in an office on the site of the disused and abandoned British Alkali Works near Birmingham where his father had been manager. At Lincoln, with far more appropriate internal architecture, he was able to fashion a pleasing space. Reached from the drawing room by means of three steps of a short winding staircase, the oratory was a long, narrow room dominated by the three lights of the stained-glass window Arthur described as consisting of 'our Lord crowned and robed on the cross; on either side the Virgin Mother and St John' and bearing the legend '*Renovabitur ut aquila juventus tua*' ('Thy youth shall be renewed like the eagle'). Family prayers were said here morning and evening, with an additional Compline on Sundays. On Wednesdays and Sundays the Litany was taken from Benson's own translation from the Greek. Musical accompaniment on these occasions was provided by Minnie on the compact harmonium picked up by her thrifty husband for £5 from a Lincoln market stall, its tremulous tones brought to life on the miniature keyboard that consisted of only three octaves. Designed for its portability, it was prone to collapse, and interruptions to prayers for mechanical adjustment were common. Benson converted the ancient chapel into a schoolroom because education, alongside prayer, was to be at the centre of life at the Chancery.

Social life for the Chancellor and his wife was not as full as it had been at Wellington. As a couple they were sociable but not gregarious. Evenings were occasionally spent out; Minnie at the newly created musical gathering of ladies who met once a week or so to play what Fred remembered as 'easy Bach' to each other. On other occasions it was the Victorian equivalent of the book club – something Arthur referred to as her 'Essay and Discussion Society'. Edward, meanwhile, was immersed in the establishment and running of the new theological college. The duties of the Chancellor were not onerous: he was legally required to reside in Lincoln for three months, preach once each Sunday, and hold lectures in the Chapter House. But for a man with Benson's energy and drive, spiritual, educational and philanthropic duties went far beyond the specified obligations. A temperance society was set up, university extension classes established, as well as a night school to educate the labouring poor. Notwithstanding the importance he attached to self-discipline and his inability, according to his children, to enjoy himself, there was the occasional festal night in the Chancery. On these memorable occasions one of the boys might be invited to accompany their father down to the 'dungeon', 'a brick-paved vaulted cellar with solid wooden pillars, lit by glimmering loopholes on a level with the pavement'. Arthur recalled acting as sacristan – a 'delicious privilege' – assisting his father in decanting the port by the light of a solitary candle in this 'fungus-lined, dusk-scented' underworld.

The children had been tutored well and their father's scholarly expectations were high. In such an intense domestic atmosphere there was ample opportunity for debate and informed conversation outside the school-room. On nights when Benson was not busy with his working-men's Bible class or at the theological college, he liked nothing better than to sit in the panelled drawing room with its big oriel window, the image of the Victorian patriarch, his wife and children gathered around him, reading, discussing, playing cards or Floral Lotto. On closer inspection, however, all was not quite as perfect as it seemed, perhaps symbolized by the broken fireplace pediment on which stood a blue china vase that was, in fact, only half a vase, with a flat white back, hidden from view. The room's tapping ghost was another, unacknowledged, ominous presence in this picture of familial happiness.

There were cracks discernible in this image of matrimonial harmony, however. Minnie was struggling with her own demons; Benson himself was deeply depressed and was an austere and distant figure both to his wife, whom he bullied, and to his children. Arthur observed: 'We feared my father's constant scrutiny and occasional displeasure very much, and indeed did little to provoke either. What was certainly hidden from me at the time was the passionate depth of his affection for us, and the overwhelming anxiety which the smallest sign of moral indolence would evoke in him.' Fred shared this view: 'With him we were careful to be decorous to the verge of woodenness. We had washed hands and neat hair and low voices, because thus we minimized the risks of his society … We sat on the edge of our chairs, and were glad to be gone.'

One family custom took the form of a poetic challenge around the dining-room table. At breakfast, the children, eagerly anticipating the deliciousness of a warm roll, would have to come up with a rhyming couplet in order to gain this coveted prize. One of the nascent poet Arthur's more memorable offerings was: 'Roll hither, roll, and let the word be said,/Which gives my palate something more than bread.' He later surmised that this may have been the high-water mark. When the rules were explained to the visiting Frederick Temple, who would succeed their father as Archbishop of Canterbury, he shook his head and stretched out his hands, eyes closed. Nothing was given to him until finally he delivered the lines: 'An egg/I beg', a miserable effusion that, as Arthur observed, 'we all considered unworthy of a Bishop'.

If Minnie's sitting room, a space later occupied by Esther de Waal, was her refuge, the attic was the Benson children's domain. This was where they would compose their stories and articles for their own version of the *Saturday Review*, a London weekly paper, called the *Saturday Magazine*, a family publication in the long tradition of clerical children's attic productions. Up here were the day nursery and night nursery, which Fred shared with Hugh and Beth, their nurse. Fred also had a room of his own, next door to the nursery, of which he was territorially proud despite it being uninhabitable, piled up with boxes and 'always shrouded in deadly gloom'. Having this room gave him 'a sense of pomp and dignity', but he was robbed of it when his father rearranged the attic floor. Benson, not a man to be defeated by the laws of architecture – as Bishop of Truro he would construct his own cathedral – devised an ingenious method of linking the front and back attic rooms via a passage across the roof. This saved the elderly Beth a long hike down to the front door and up the staircase on the other side of the house in order to reach the older children's bedrooms from the nursery. Edward Benson, with his usual eye and ear for apposite naming, christened the passage 'the Rialto'.

The Chancellor had created what his children came to view as 'very comfortable habitations' up on their third floor. Whitewashed and well papered, they were very livable, but no amount of even his inventive alterations could press the curious layout and erratic shapes of the rooms into uniformity. It was a world of untamed inconsistencies, irregular spaces and winding stairs – making it the perfect place for a frightening form of hide-and-seek. It was a thrillingly terrifying ordeal for the children to come across a body in a gloomy attic corner and, despite knowing it to be that of a sibling, still be able to revel in the *frisson* of the possibility that the being was the incarnation of a hobgoblin, some form of non-human come to life from its hiding place in the attic's gurgling water cistern.

The Chancery garden also offered hiding places, especially among the tall grasses of the overgrown asparagus beds. There were numerous paths of discovery that led to inner and outer gardens; grassy banks made for rolling down; two ancient ivy-covered towers (part of the old city fortifications); limestone-walled arches revealing rich orchards; and, beyond, a lawn large enough for rounders and the new game of tennis on a court somewhat eccentrically marked out by tape fixed in place with hairpins. A mysterious Roman sarcophagus, rescued from a building site by Benson and containing the bones of two children, stood in a corner. In the inner garden a surpliced Benson would walk for hours, carrying his notebook, composing his sermons. His children would often see him in his favourite position up on a steep grassy mound, a perfect spot from which to survey his parish.

Minnie, who admitted much later that she never grew up, joined in the children's games, such as Knight's A-Three. She was also adjudicator for the terrifying game of Sieges, conducted up the steep narrow stairs of one of the ruined towers in the garden. They lived in an enclosed world, with its own rules and erratic intricacies that the children never quite solved. Hidden turret stairs in one of the towers were supposed to lead to a neighbour's garden, but this was never tested as the ground-floor room contained a deep stone

The Chancery, now the Deanery, at Lincoln, viewed from the garden. The mixture of architectural styles reflects the building's long history.

shaft that had nearly swallowed one of the boys on the first and only visit to this sinister location.

In the attic a big empty room was given to the children by their father 'with which we were allowed to deal precisely as we wished'. It was instantly called 'The Museum' and became the storehouse for souvenirs of childhood wanderings, a repository for the fragments of unknown and ancient worlds. Maggie found a strand of sheep's wool in a hedge and this was brought back, washed white, combed and placed in a cardboard box with a glass lid. One day their mother killed a hornet and the corpse was delivered reverentially to 'The Museum' where it was preserved in a large bowl of water the children had lined with spa and madrepore (fossils and coral) from their collection. An addled swan's egg was also conserved, but after the smell of its putrefying contents became overwhelming it was reluctantly discarded. Armed with a set of geological hammers, gifts from their father, the children dug up fossils, brightly coloured pieces of oxydized glass, and the broken bowls and stems of tobacco pipes. The older the item from the dig the better – it was the palpable patina of age that appealed most to these young collectors. For the Benson offspring the gift of their father's fine stamp collection was considered 'rather dull: the hornet disintegrating in the bread-bowl, and the piece of sheep's wool were far more interesting,' as Fred recalled. The objects 'had the timbre of personal acquisition, and rang with first-hand emotion'.

To Fred, the time at the Chancery appeared 'to have lasted for decades', but one morning in 1877, after only three and a half years in Lincoln, Benson was standing in his dressing room, from where he could see into the room where the post was laid out. There were two letters on the table and he recalled being struck by the sense that they contained momentous information. One was from the Prime Minister, Lord Beaconsfield, the recently ennobled Benjamin Disraeli, offering him the bishopric of the newly created see of Truro, the other was from Queen Victoria, urging him to accept; the offer was a 'bombshell', according to Fred, that 'blew Lincoln into fragments'.

Almost a century later, in August 1969, another Chancellor, Victor de Waal, arrived at the Chancery with his wife, Esther, and their four small sons. The eldest, John, was 7, Alexander 6, Edmund would celebrate his fifth birthday the month after their arrival, and Thomas, the youngest, was just 3. Their previous house in Nottingham, where Victor had been university chaplain, had been a mock-Tudor building on the edge of the campus. Their new home was a

Grade I listed building where the Tudor elements might be considered comparatively modern and its unexpected spaces, hidden nooks, myriad staircases and labyrinthine corridors constructed at different periods could not have offered more of a contrast to where they had lived before.

Coming from a house with modern central heating, the Chancery was 'very, very cold', so much so that Esther would sometimes take the two younger boys their breakfast porridge in bed so they could start their day in comparative warmth, and the bright red blankets added to the cosy feel. With three outside walls, the temperature in the kitchen was bitter in winter and everyone dressed in layers. Esther always wore a long skirt over a flannel petticoat and 'everyone envied Victor wrapped up in his cloak of office sweeping out of the house in timeless fashion'.

Esther felt well prepared for life in the Chancery as her father was a vicar. She had been brought up in draughty and unheated country vicarages in Shropshire and Herefordshire and was undaunted by the extensive house and garden at Lincoln. As the four boys tumbled through the ancient portal, John, as the eldest, was given first choice of room and decided upon one up the spiral staircase that still carried the original masons' marks. It was here that he established 'The Museum' – only later did he discover that this very space had been assigned to the same purpose by the Benson children.

Edmund discovered his own secret history of touch at Lincoln. Esther's father had not only been a vicar but also an antiquarian and medieval historian, and bringing the past into the present via tangible objects was part of her hinterland of experience. Together with John, they conducted their own archaeological dig in the Chancery garden where they collected oyster shells, Georgian pennies and fragments of pottery and clay pipes and, like the Benson children, such treasures were transported with great seriousness to 'The Museum'. An elderly archdeacon at the cathedral had collected fossils and these he passed on to Edmund, a passionate collector himself from a young age. These fossils were kept, alongside treasures from the digs, in a large vitrine in the bedroom he shared with Thomas. There was space here to pursue whatever was the current enthusiasm – playing with the old archdeacon's lead soldiers, an additional collection passed on to the de Waal offspring, or taking the precious fossils out of their glass case and endlessly arranging and rearranging them. Just as 'The Museum' had been for the Benson children, these collections formed Edmund's *Wunderkammer*. To him the objects were a narrative of loss

The de Waal family at the door of the Chancery, 1969. Esther and Victor stand behind with, from left to right, Thomas, John, Edmund and Alexander.

The vast interior of Lincoln Cathedral. 'Containing birth and death, potential with all the noise and transition of life,' D. H. Lawrence wrote of it in *The Rainbow*.

and rediscovery, like the netsuke in his widely acclaimed family memoir *The Hare with Amber Eyes* (2010).

Touch exuded a powerful influence on the young Edmund, and these years of digging and handling precious objects might be considered part of the genesis of his career as a potter. His first pottery offering was a small, dumpy bowl he insisted be painted monastic white. 'Everyone else was writing,' he later recalled. 'Making was me trying to make a different identity for myself.' From his wanderings in the Fens with his mother he also learned the importance of not touching. Esther was attending botany classes and shared this new interest with Edmund on local field trips with experts who would lead them to hidden places to admire the fragility and shape of a Green-winged Orchid. Both savoured these moments of standing back.

Edmund was not the only de Waal son who experimented with making, however. When the local art college opened its doors on Thursday evenings everyone had an opportunity to discover what they wanted to do. Along with Edmund's feeling for pots, it was here that his older brother Alexander was encouraged to draw. Esther remembers him producing small exquisite sketches and watercolours, training that made him much in demand in theatre design later at Oxford. He had his own creative space in his chosen room at the other end of the house above the chapel. An attic led out of the room and here he carefully crafted models of ships, railway stations and even whole villages with medieval churches. Georgian and Victorian architectural styles were all replicated down to the finest detail of brick and tile, a considerable feat considering they were constructed mainly from cornflake packets. John and Thomas also painted and most of them wrote – stories, poems and plays. Victor, the Chancellor, like his predecessor Benson a century before, was engaged in promoting education in the cathedral, diocese and county. Much of his time was taken up with teaching at the theological college (called since Benson's day Scholae Cancelarii) and with the further education of the clergy, but he also preached and lectured in the cathedral and cared for its magnificent library.

The proximity of the cathedral engendered a familiarity with the vocabulary of architecture among all the de Waals. Esther, who had been taught this language by her father, passed on to her children the mysteries of clerestory and triforium and an appreciation for the skills and artistry of the medieval masons and the intricacy of the choir vaulting. They were taught to see and interpret architecture, to discover hidden layers of texture. From a distance, Lincoln seems a solid structure like its muscular counterpart at Durham, but on closer inspection more delicate elements and tracery are revealed.

Every form of creative and imaginative activity was encouraged within the Chancery. Esther was fiercely determined not to have television – although the boys were allowed to go and watch a couple of programmes with a neighbour. One of these was 'Blue Peter', an inspirational programme for generations of children who were encouraged to mould and shape their own worlds with materials from the kitchen cupboard. Major football matches were also sanctioned television viewing and the boys would line up at the great wooden double doors waiting impatiently for the signal that it was time to go. This stimulating atmosphere produced inventive adaptations of board games, too: John improved on Monopoly with 'Ecclesia', in which cathedrals were property to be bought and sold.

Just as with the Bensons, the Tudor Great Chamber or drawing room with its oriel window was the venue for splendid gatherings and diverse debate, including talks on everything from Byzantine icons to travel in the Himalayas (this was given by Penelope Betjeman), and musical evenings. Plays were put on here, such as a week-long production by the theological college of Robert Bolt's *A Man for All Seasons* that played to a capacity audience of fifty each night. Thomas begged to be allowed to stay up for the final performance to see if Thomas More's head would really be cut off this time.

Esther remembers the Chancery as a magical place. 'Its space, and the texture of wood and stone, with window casements and the vast stained-glass window at the top of the main staircase provided different kinds of spaces which in turn led to differing reactions.' And, of course, life in the cathedral close involved a rich range of characters: eccentric cathedral canons and students from the theological college, including a young Richard Chartres (appointed Bishop of London in 1995) who taught the de Waal boys poker as well as ancient Greek. Another popular student babysitter had been a funeral director and was a source of invaluable information about corpses and the speed at which hearses raced home after funerals. There was a geologist on hand, too, to help with the fossils, and someone might bring along a trumpet for a little musical entertainment.

In such a place the past is always present. Not only through the continual prayers in the cathedral and the traditional observances, such as the tolling of the great bell for the passing of members of the cathedral community, but also through the connection with the Chancery's former inhabitants. Esther remembers one visitor asking the boys: "'And who are these Bensons whom you seem to know so well?" For they were indeed familiar.' They knew what rooms they had used, where they had buried their cat, Rector, and the Latin rhyme on the plaque. They were aware of the eccentric tennis games and followed the same passageways in their endless games of hide-and-seek. This was because on Sunday evenings Esther would read aloud from the Benson family memoirs – *The Trefoil* and *Our Family Affairs* – an echo of Minnie Benson reading Dickens to her children in front of the same fireplace a hundred years earlier.

For the de Waal boys it was a childhood that at first sight is steeped in cricket and sacred music, entirely appropriate associations for children of the chancery as they are for children of the rectory. Yet even here, deep in the heart of the Church establishment (and more scrutinized than in the rural rectory), lies the unexpected and unrevealed. The Revd Dr Victor de Waal, Chancellor and subsequently Dean of Canterbury, had Jewish ancestry. He acknowledged this at his mother's Church of England Requiem Mass, conducted in Monmouth, by including the Kaddish prayer.

Assimilation and exploration are intrinsic to the very fabric of the building itself and every member of the de Waal family, like the Bensons before them, was free to pursue their own interests and enthusiasms under the protection of the Chancery's architectural inconsistencies. Their future paths have taken them far from the safe and ritualized environment of the Established Church, however, although all agree, as their mother writes, that the Chancery played a significant part in shaping the creativity of their older years. John is now a barrister, Alexander a prolific writer on African affairs, scholar and executive director of the World Peace Foundation, Edmund a ceramicist and writer, and Thomas is also a writer and academic specializing in Russia and the Caucasus region. They are all linked by their childhood at Lincoln: 'You cannot live in this place and not be changed by it,' Esther observes.

For the Bensons, the unfolding world of the Chancery was revisited in later years by Arthur and Fred and reconstructed as a prosperous, harmless place of innocence, even if behind the mask of respectability and order there had been bitter conflict, depression and unhappiness within their parents' marriage. This paradoxical picture of the ordered clerical living masking interior struggles mirrors the experience of the Tennysons, who suffered from the instability and violence emanating from their father that was concealed behind the façade of the rectory at Somersby. In both cases the children would find the transition to the outside world problematic: none of the Benson children ever married and there were bouts of insanity, as with the Tennyson offspring.

Nonetheless, despite these examples of the harsh reality of rectory life, the dreamlike idyll of the clerical home persists. It is a myth perpetuated by those who have lived and suffered a strictured existence within its walls as well as by those who have found its imaginative pull irresistible. Thus A. C. Benson's recollection of life at the Chancery at Lincoln as having the beauty of a 'serene romance' was taken up by his acquaintance Rupert Brooke at Grantchester, where the poet set out to live this romance, not just dream or write about it. It is hard to realize and maintain the ideal, however, as Brooke discovered, although he immortalized the vision for future generations in his poem 'The Old Vicarage, Grantchester'. John Betjeman attempted to create a life reminiscent of those lived by earlier occupants of the Old Rectory at Farnborough yet he too was forced to admit defeat when his marriage foundered. He moved on to fight for his vision of England, much of it rooted in church architecture and rural landscapes under threat, and gave it voice in his poetry and broadcasts from the comfort of his secular homes in London and Trebetherick in Cornwall.

For the Revd Sydney Smith, on the other hand, in his working rectory at Foston, the contentment was palpable. He rose to the challenges of his isolated parish, creating for himself a perfectly parsonic parsonage, just 'like those described in novels', as he wryly observed. Indeed, Smith was possibly the basis of Jane Austen's hero Henry Tilney in *Northanger Abbey*, as she might have met him at Bath in 1797. Smith recognized his own and the Church's limitations but adapted himself and his outlook to work within their confines. He was, perhaps, fortunate, and a product of his time. The parish in the early nineteenth century was yet to be plagued by doubt and dwindling congregations; the rector's position was secure.

By the time R. S. Thomas was established in his Church in Wales rectory at Manafon, however, the paradisal dream of rectory living was detectable only to his wife, Elsi. With her artist's eye she could appreciate its Eden-like elements and translate them into her art, combining her ability to capture detail with a mythical vision that resulted in murals on an epic scale, as well as more intimate works. Meanwhile, her husband strode the hillsides, seeking an authentic poetic voice with which to engage with the Welsh people and his native land, a quest that took him ever westwards, never quite at peace.

Today, the romance of the rectory persists, even if the example of the lives of some of the characters in this story is not an entirely happy one. Behind parsonage walls lurk hidden desires, domestic dramas, bitterness and isolation. Yet this tension of opposites, so particularly fitting in the religious context of a rectory, has proved to be highly creative for some of Britain's best-known authors. For them, the point where private passions and public probity converge could be enormously productive and, by means of their writing, positively resolved.

'Some houses are built like fictions, and are even built of fictions,' the author and critic Malcolm Bradbury wrote of Shandy Hall, the Revd Laurence Sterne's vicarage in Coxwold, North Yorkshire. The rectory is one such place. Not only have rectory children created their own fictional worlds but also those writers drawn to inhabit the same spaces. In these instances, the sacramental importance of creativity is both nurtured and sanctioned.

The picturesque rectory neighbouring an ancient church in a timeless village has a more profound role in the national psyche than this sentimental image might suggest. As Henry James, that great observer of English life, wrote in *English Hours* (1905) of Wenlock Abbey in Shropshire: 'This entertainment is inexhaustible; for every step you take in such a house confronts you in one way or another with the remote past. You devour the documentary, you inhale the historic.' As many of the country's finest writers and poets have discovered, the rectory provides a link between what we were, what we are and what we will become – it is a place that borders on the numinous, where we can, in E. M. Forster's famous epigraph to *Howards End* (1910), 'Only connect'.

Bibliography

In the relevant chapters, manuscript sources are followed by printed sources.

GENERAL

Bachelard, Gaston, *The Poetics of Space*, trans. by Maria Jolas. New York, 1964

Bax, B. Anthony, *The English Parsonage*. London, 1964

Blunden, Edmund, *The Face of England, in a Series of Occasional Sketches*. London and New York, 1932

Blythe, Ronald, *Divine Landscapes*. London, 1986

Drabble, Margaret, *A Writer's Britain: Landscapes in Literature*. London, 1979; 2nd edn, 2009

Giles, Judy and Tim Middleton (eds), *Writing Englishness 1900–1950: An Introductory Sourcebook on National Identity*. London and New York, 1995

Harris, Alexandra, *Romantic Moderns: English Writers, Artists and the Imagination from Virginia Woolf to John Piper*. London and New York, 2010

Hill, Rosemary, *God's Architect: Pugin and the Building of Romantic Britain*. London, 2007

Jennings, Anthony, *The Old Rectory: The Story of the English Parsonage*. London, 2009

Jones, Anthea, *A Thousand Years of the English Parish: Medieval Patterns and Modern Interpretations*. Moreton-in-Marsh, 2000

Kilvert, Robert Francis, *Kilvert's Diary, 1870–1879*, edited by William Plomer. London, 1944

Marsh, Kate (ed.), *Writers and their Houses: A Guide to the Writers' Houses of England, Scotland, Wales and Ireland*. London, 1993

Morton, H. V., *In Search of England*. London, 1927

Savidge, Alan, *The Parsonage in England: Its History and Architecture*. London, 1964

Short, Brian (ed.), *The English Rural Community: Image and Analysis*. Cambridge and New York, 1992

Skinner, John, *Journal of a Somerset Rector, 1803–1834*, edited by Howard and Peter Coombs. London, 1930; revd edn, Bath, 1971

Strong, Roy, *Visions of England*. London, 2011

INTRODUCTION
University of Sussex, Monk's House Papers

Brontë, Charlotte, *The Letters of Charlotte Brontë*, edited by Margaret Smith, 3 vols. Oxford, 1995–2004

Cobbett, William, *Rural Rides*, edited by George Woodcock. Harmondsworth, 1967

Collins, Irene, *Jane Austen and the Clergy*. London, 1994

Cowper, William, *Cowper: Poetical Works*, edited by H. S. Milford. 4th edn, Oxford, 1964

Eliot, George, *Scenes of Clerical Life*. Edinburgh and London, 1858; London, 1998

Eliot, T. S., *The Complete Poems and Plays*. London, 1969

Gaskell, Elizabeth, *The Life of Charlotte Brontë*. London, 1857

Halfpenny, William, *Useful Architecture in Twenty-one New Designs for Country Parsonages, Farm Houses and Inns*. London, 1752

Noon, Charles, *Parson Jack Russell: The Hunting Legend*. Tiverton, 2000

Priestley, J. B., *English Journey*. London, 1934

Ruskin, John, *The Seven Lamps of Architecture*. 1849; New York, 1989

Thomas, Edward, *Collected Poems*. London, 1936; London, 2004

Trollope, Anthony, *Clergymen of the Church of England*. London, 1866; Leicester, 1974

Woolf, Virginia
—, *The Diary of Virginia Woolf*, Vol. I, *1915–1919*, edited by Anne Olivier Bell, assisted by Andrew McNeillie. London, 1977
—, *The Essays of Virginia Woolf*, edited by Andrew McNeillie (Vols 1–4) and Stuart N. Clarke (Vols 5–6). London, 1986–2011

CHAPTER ONE
Borthwick Institute, University of York; Castle Howard Archives, York

Bell, Alan, *Sydney Smith*. Oxford and New York, 1980

Holland, Saba, Lady, *A Memoir of the Reverend Sydney Smith*, 2 vols. 4th edn, London, 1855

Pearson, Hesketh, *The Smith of Smiths: Being the Life, Wit and Humour of Sydney Smith*. London, 1934; new edn, 2009

Smith, Sydney, *The Letters of Sydney Smith*, edited by Nowell C. Smith, 2 vols. Oxford, 1953

—, *Selected Writings of Sydney Smith*, edited by W. H. Auden. New York, 1956, London, 1957

—, *The Works of the Rev. Sydney Smith*. London, 1850

CHAPTER TWO
Tennyson Research Centre, Lincoln Central Library, Lincolnshire County Council

Rawnsley, H. D., *Memories of the Tennysons*. Glasgow, 1900; 2nd edn, 1912

Ricks, Chirstopher, *Tennyson*. London and New York, 1972

Tennyson, Alfred, *Poems by Two Brothers*. 1827; 2nd edn, London and New York, 1893

—, *The Poems of Tennyson*, edited by Christopher Ricks. London, 1969

—, *Unpublished Early Poems*, edited by Charles Tennyson. London, 1931

—, *The Works of Tennyson: With Notes by the Author*, edited by Hallam, Lord Tennyson. London, 1913

Tennyson, Charles, *Alfred Tennyson and Somersby*. Lincoln, 1962; revd edn, 1974

—, *Alfred Tennyson: By his Grandson Charles Tennyson*. London, 1949

Tennyson, Charles and Hope Dyson, *The Tennysons: Background to Genius*. London, 1974

Tennyson, Hallam, *Alfred, Lord Tennyson: A Memoir by his Son*, 2 vols. London and New York, 1897

Wheatcroft, Andrew, *The Tennyson Album: A Biography in Original Photographs*. London, 1980

CHAPTER THREE
Auden, W. H., 'The Guilty Vicarage', in *The Complete Works of W. H. Auden, Prose*, Vol. 4, *1956–1962*, edited by Edward Mendelson. Princeton, NJ, 2010

Reynolds, Barbara, *Dorothy L. Sayers: Her Life and Soul*. London, 1993; 3rd edn, 2002

Sayers, Dorothy L., *Dorothy L. Sayers: Child and Woman of her Time, A Supplement to The Letters of Dorothy L. Sayers*, Vol. 5, edited by Barbara Reynolds. Swavesey, 2002

—, *The Letters of Dorothy L. Sayers*. Vol. 1, *1899–1936: The Making of a Detective Novelist*, edited by Barbara Reynolds, with a preface by P. D. James. London, 1995

—, *The Nine Tailors*. London, 1934

CHAPTER FOUR
Archer, Mary, *Rupert Brooke and the Old Vicarage, Grantchester*. Cambridge, 1989

—, *The Story of the Old Vicarage, Grantchester*. Cambridge, 2012

Brooke, Rupert, *The Collected Poems of Rupert Brooke, With a Memoir [by Edward Marsh]*. 7th impression, London, 1920

—, *The Letters of Rupert Brooke*, edited by Geoffrey Keynes. London and New York, 1968

Delany, Paul, *The Neo-Pagans: Friendship and Love in the Rupert Brooke Circle*. London, 1987

Garnett, David, *The Golden Echo*. London, 1953

Hassall, Christopher, *Edward Marsh, Patron of the Arts: A Biography*. London and New York, 1959

—, *Rupert Brooke: A Biography*. London, 1964

Hastings, Michael, *The Handsomest Young Man in England: Rupert Brooke*. London, 1967

Jennings, Christine, *Widnall, A Capital Contriver: The Story of a Victorian Household in the Village of Grantchester*. Swavesey, 2003

Keynes, Geoffrey, *The Gates of Memory: No Life is Long Enough*. Oxford and New York, 1981

Lehmann, John, *Rupert Brooke: His Life and his Legend*. London, 1980

CHAPTER FIVE
Betjeman, John, *Archie and the Strict Baptists*. London, 1977

—, *Coming Home, An Anthology of his Prose, 1920–1977*, selected by Candida Lycett Green. London, 1997

—, *Faith and Doubt of John Betjeman: An Anthology of Betjeman's Religious Verse*, edited by Kevin J. Gardner. London, 2005

—, *A Few Late Chrysanthemums*. London, 1954

—, *Ghastly Good Taste, or, A Depressing Story of the Rise and Fall of English Architecture*. London, 1933; 3rd edn, 1986

—, *High and Low*. London, 1966

—, *John Betjeman Letters*, Vol. 1, *1926–1951*, edited by Candida Lycett Green. London, 1994

——, *Old Lights for New Chancels: Verses Topographical and Amatory*. London, 1940

——, *Poems in the Porch*. London, 1956

——, *Slick but not Streamlined: Poems and Short Pieces*, selected by W. H. Auden. Garden City, New York, 1947

——, *Summoned by Bells*. London, 1960

Betjeman, John with Paul Hogarth, *In Praise of Churches*. London, 1996

Hillier, Bevis, *John Betjeman: The Biography*. London, 2006

——, *John Betjeman: A Life in Pictures*. London, 1984

——, *John Betjeman: New Fame, New Love*. London, 2002

Lycett Green, Candida, *The Dangerous Edge of Things*. London, 2005

Lycett Green, Imogen, *Grandmother's Footsteps: A Journey in Search of Penelope Betjeman*. London, 1994

Waugh, Evelyn, *The Diaries of Evelyn Waugh*, edited by Michael Davie. London, 1976

——, *The Letters of Evelyn Waugh*, edited by Mark Amory. London, 1980

Wilson, A. N., *Betjeman*. London and New York, 2006

Woodward, George, *A Parson in the Vale of White Horse: George Woodward's Letters from East Hendred, 1753–1761*, edited Donald Gibson. Gloucester, 1982

CHAPTER SIX

R. S. Thomas Study Centre, Bangor University

Brown, Tony, *R. S. Thomas*. Cardiff, 2006

Davies, Damian Walford (ed.), *Echoes to the Amen: Essays after R. S. Thomas*. Cardiff, 2003

Larkin, Philip, *Selected Letters of Philip Larkin, 1940–1985*, edited by Anthony Thwaite. London, 1992

Rogers, Byron, *The Man Who Went into the West: The Life of R. S. Thomas*. London, 2006

Thomas R. S., *Autobiographies*, trans. by Jason Walford Davies. London, 1997

——, *Collected Later Poems, 1988–2000*. Tarset, 2004

——, *Collected Poems, 1945–1990*. London, 1993

——, *Neb*. Caernarfon, 1985

——, *Song at the Year's Turning: Poems 1942–1954*. London, 1955

Wintle, Justin, *Furious Interiors: Wales, R. S. Thomas and God*. London, 1996

CHAPTER SEVEN

Charles, Amy M., *A Life of George Herbert*. Ithaca, NY, 1977

Herbert, George, *The English Poems of George Herbert*, edited by Helen Wilcox. Cambridge and New York, 2007

——, *A Priest to the Temple or The Country Parson*, edited by Ronald Blythe. Norwich, 2003

——, *The Works of George Herbert*, edited by F. E. Hutchinson. Oxford, 1941

Seth, Vikram, *The Rivered Earth*. London, 2011

Walton, Izaak, *Life of George Herbert*. London, 1670; 2012

CHAPTER EIGHT

Bodleian Library, University of Oxford, Papers of the Benson Family, Mary Benson Diaries; Pepys Library, Magdalene College, University of Cambridge, A. C. Benson Diaries

Benson, A. C., *The Life of Edward White Benson, Sometime Archbishop of Canterbury*, 2 vols. London and New York, 1899

——, *Mary Benson: A Memoir*. 1891; Rye, 2010

——, *The Trefoil: Wellington College, Lincoln, and Truro*. London, 1923

Benson, E. F., *Our Family Affairs 1867–1896*, London and New York, 1920

Bolt, Rodney, *As Good as God, as Clever as the Devil: The Impossible Life of Mary Benson*. London, 2011

de Waal, Edmund, *The Hare with Amber Eyes: A Hidden Inheritance*. London, 2010

de Waal, Esther, *Living on the Border: Connecting Inner and Outer Worlds*. Norwich, 2011

Lawrence, D. H., *The Rainbow*. London, 1915

Acknowledgments

I am very grateful to Fiona Inchyra for starting the ball rolling in the first place and for her good-humoured company throughout. Frances Stonor Saunders provided valuable insights and helped me to hone my ideas. I would also like to thank the many people who generously shared their thoughts on the subject of writers and rectories, including Esther de Waal, P. D. James, Charles Moore and John Walsh, as well as those associated with county and university archives and pertinent societies who were unstinting with their time, advice and encouragement: Dr Nicholas Bennett for his historical insights on Lincoln; Professor Tony Brown at Bangor University; Grace Cummins at the Tennyson Research Centre; Seona Ford, Chairman of the Dorothy L. Sayers Society; Gwydion and Kunjana Thomas; and Anne Trevett of the Bemerton Historical Society who shared her considerable knowledge and was kind enough to introduce me to Alec Roth. The Rectory Society gave sturdy support to the project and to everyone there, especially Alison Everington, I owe a great debt. I am also thankful to the late Major Peter Diggle who made room for a few extra guests at his entertaining lunch for the Sydney Smith Society in York.

I was privileged to have been warmly welcomed through the 'ever-open' door of so many of these former rectories and vicarages by their current incumbents. Michael and Caroline Todhunter were especially generous, but I would also like to record my appreciation of David Carson and James and Sarah Walsh. Dame Mary Archer was kind enough to reward my curiosity by offering me coffee cake and sharing her detailed knowledge of the Old Vicarage, Grantchester. She also introduced me to Lady Christine Jennings, herself an authority on life at the OV before Rupert Brooke. Miss Rosemary Puxley gave me delightful descriptions of life at Farnborough. The Very Reverend Philip Buckler, Dean of Lincoln, allowed me to explore the former Chancery. A previous resident, Edmund de Waal, gave an inspiring talk to the Rectory Society that alerted me to Lincoln's rich literary associations.

Rectory-crawling around the country has meant relying on the hospitality of many friends. I give them all my thanks, but in particular Claire and James Birch, Sir Christopher and Lady Ondaatje and Jans Ondaatje Rolls. Tom Woolfenden helped me enormously, Martin Bunting took the time to add his perceptive observations on John Betjeman, and Archie Cotterill kept on reading and made me laugh. My gratitude also goes to Kate Shemilt for her wonderful photography.

I would like to thank the team at Thames & Hudson as well as Mary-Jane Gibson for her support, expertise and thoughtful approach to the picture research.

Above all, to my boys (large and small), who have borne the brunt of my single-mindedness and obsessive research, I say an enormous thank you. This book is dedicated to you.

I would like to thank the following for permission to quote work in copyright:

Extracts from the works of John Betjeman Copyright © John Betjeman by permission of The Estate of John Betjeman.

'Church Going' taken from *The Complete Poems* Copyright © Estate of Philip Larkin and reprinted by permission of Faber and Faber Ltd.

David Higham Associates for Dorothy L. Sayers.

Penguin Books for permission to quote from *The Rivered Earth* by Vikram Seth (Hamish Hamilton, 2011). Copyright © Vikram Seth, 2011.

Bloodaxe Books for permission to quote from 'At the End' and 'Manafon' by R. S. Thomas, *Collected Later Poems, 1988–2000* (Bloodaxe, 2004). All other extracts from the works of R. S. Thomas Copyright © Kunjana Thomas 2001.

Extract from Volume I: 1915–1919 of *The Diary of Virginia Woolf*, edited by Anne Olivier Bell, published by The Hogarth Press. Reprinted by permission of The Random House Group Limited.

Extract from 'Two Parsons' taken from Volume V: 1929–1932 of *The Essays of Virginia Woolf*, edited by Stuart N. Clarke, published by The Hogarth Press. Reprinted by permission of The Random House Group Limited.

Extract from 'White's Selborne' taken from Volume VI: 1933–1941 of *The Essays of Virginia Woolf*, edited by Stuart N. Clarke, published by The Hogarth Press. Reprinted by permission of The Random House Group Limited.

Picture Credits

Frontispiece Photo © Country Life; **6** Eric Ravilious, frontispiece to *The Writings of Gilbert White of Selborne*, London, Nonesuch Press, 1938; **9** Photo Brontë Parsonage Museum/Bridgeman Art Library; **16** Photo Royal College of Surgeons; **17** Photo King's College Library, Cambridge/RCB/Ph; **19** Photo Grainger Collection/Topfoto; **25** Borthwick Institute, University of York; **28** Photo Deborah Alun-Jones; **29** Courtesy of The Duke of Abercorn, photo Bryan Rutledge; **31** Castle Howard Collection reproduced by courtesy of the Hon. Simon Howard; **33** Wheelwright from *The Book of English Trades and The Library of Useful Arts*, 1824; **35** Private Collection; **39** Abbot Hall Art Gallery, Cumbria/Bridgeman Art Library; **40, 43** Private Collection; **44** Photo A. F. Kersting; **51, 52, 58, 59, 61** Tennyson Research Centre, Lincoln Central Library; **55** Private Collection; **65** Reproduced with the permission of Dr Barbara Reynolds © Norah Lambourne; **68** Photo Paul Whitehead, MM Photographic, Cambridge; **69** Photo James P. Miller; **71, 72** Mrs Fortuna Fleming; **75** Revd Colin Backhouse; **77, 78, 82** Used by permission of The Marion Wade Center, Wheaton College, Wheaton, Illinois; **85** Estate of Anthony Fleming by permission of David Higham; **89** Private Collection; **93, 94** Photos Charlie Ward; **97, 98, 100, 101, 104** Photos King's College Library, Cambridge/RCB/Ph; **111** Photo Betjeman Family Archives; **112** © Estate of Osbert Lancaster by permission of Clare Hastings; **115** Photo National Portrait Gallery, London; **118** Photo courtesy Candida Lycett Green; **122** Photo Edwin Smith; **124** Photo National Portrait Gallery, London; **125** Photo Betjeman Family Archives; **126** Photo National Portrait Gallery, London; **129** © Estate of John Piper, photo Country Life; **135, 144, 145** By permission of Gwydion Thomas © Kunjana Thomas, 2001; **136** Abbott & Holder by permission of Gwydion Thomas © Kunjana Thomas, 2001; **139** R. S. Thomas Study Centre, Bangor University; **140** Photo Martin Crampin; **148, 153** R. S. Thomas Study Centre, Bangor University by permission of Gwydion Thomas © Kunjana Thomas, 2001; **154** Photo Jane Bown/Topfoto; **157** Photo Kate Shemilt; **160** Photo Deborah Alun-Jones; **163** Frontispiece to *The English Works of George Herbert*, *Volume 1*, London, Hodder & Stoughton, 1905; **166** Photo The George Herbert in Bemerton Group; **169** From an 1876 facsimile reprint of the 1st edition of *The Temple, Sacred Poems and Private Ejaculations* by George Herbert, 1633; **170** Guildhall Art Gallery, City of London; **172** Photo Kate Shemilt; **176** Private Collection; **179** Photo from *The Life of Edward White Benson* by A. C. Benson, London, Macmillan, 1900; **180** Photo The de Waal Family Collection; **182, 183 (left)** Photos from *Life and Letters of Maggie Benson* by A. C. Benson, London, John Murray, 1917; **183 (right)** Photo from *E. F. Benson, As He Was* by Geoffrey Palmer and Noel Lloyd, Luton, Bedfordshire, Lennard Publishing, 1988; **188, 191** Photo The de Waal Family Collection; **192** Photo A. F. Kersting.

Index